Children's
Books
of International
Interest

Virginia Haviland

American Library
Association

Children's
Books
of International
Interest

Children's Books of International Interest

A Selection from Four Decades
of American Publishing

Virginia Haviland
Editor

American Library Association
Chicago 1972

ISBN 0-8389-0130-1 (1972)

Library of Congress Catalog Card Number 72-1161

Copyright © 1972 by the American Library Association

Printed in the United States of America

Contents

Preface

Among the aims of UNESCO for International Book Year is the improvement of the production and distribution of books through international exchange. This has been a motivating ideal, too, for children's librarians organized within the American Library Association. Since 1955, a decade and a half preceding the designation of 1972 as International Book Year, the Children's Services Division of the American Library Association, through its International Relations Committee, has expressed in a special bibliographic series its belief in the value of the international exchange of children's books. This has been the purpose of the succession of annual lists entitled *Books of International Interest* (previously entitled *Books Recommended for Translation*). Over the years these lists have been made available at international congresses—at the International Federation of Library Associations (IFLA) and at the International Board on Books for Young People (IBBY)—to librarians, publishers, booksellers, and others seeking to promote the production and distribution of good books internationally.

The role of internationalism in promoting understanding and cooperation is becoming more widely recognized in the world of children's books. The flow of books between countries and copublishing arrangements are being furthered at the Bologna Children's Book Fair as well as at the Frankfurt Book Fair. As recognition is given by means of international and other prizes, notably IBBY's Hans Christian Andersen's biennial medals, awarded since 1956 for the writing and, since 1966, for the illustration of children's books, the necessary exchange of information about good books has been intensified.

The American Library Association considered it significant as an American project for International Book Year to take a fresh, retrospective look at the children's books produced in the United States during the past four decades and at its annual lists to reevaluate the whole with the support of the test of time, to note those books superseded by later publications, and to take account of changing interests and developments in the world of children.

The initial list issued by the American Library Association in 1955 comprised 100 titles published from 1930 through 1954. The succeeding annual lists, each containing from twenty to sixty books which the committee estimated to have both literary value and universality of interest, reached a total this year of some 700 titles: picture-story books, fiction, folklore, biography, history, science, and other factual books. Long-time classics, except for a few freshly illustrated editions which thus have attained a new look, do not appear.

With the help of past committee members Barbara Moody, Isabel Wilner, Anne Pellowski, Sarah Innis Fenwick, and Della Thomas, and of Margaret N. Coughlan of the Library of Congress, the original titles were considered individually and their total number reduced to somewhat less than half for this edited summary. Some separate entries have been eliminated by combining into a single entry companion works by an author. Some titles, overlooked in the year following publication, have been newly listed on the basis of proven importance. Always the choice to retain or add a title has been based on the aim of past committees to present work which is a genuine contribution to literature for children and young people. Questions have been asked abroad about kinds of books sought for republishing. As was considered each year, picture books selected are still "recommended for consideration provided that pictures as well as story can be reproduced. Each of these books is notable because of the unity of text and pictures." The wide range of fiction represented indicates belief in the sustaining strength and universality of creative writing. The smaller proportion of nonfiction that has remained after the sifting reveals the hard fact that informational books in general have a shorter life.

Many reasons support our belief in the importance of compiling this summary list. Our purposes for the annual lists had been strengthened in 1965 by the concern that sent Mildred L. Batchelder of the American Library Association headquarters staff to Europe on a sabbatical leave to study the acceptance of our translated books. There she discovered that books far less than our best much too often found their way to other countries. The information contained in her interviews with librarians, children's book editors, and others in eleven European countries has enabled us to assess the success or lack of success of translated American books—of particular titles and also of kinds of books—and to learn what kinds of books were sought.

The present, reevaluated, stringent winnowing of the earlier selections highlights the scope and variety of American children's books. It also identifies those intrinsically excellent, enriching, and enduring works, both fiction and nonfiction, which are estimated to have interest for the world abroad. For whom? For publishers, obviously—those who have no specific critical channels established to aid them in making selections. And for their translators, who, similarly, wish to study trends and subject matter and produce editions of the best books for their own countries. For those also who disseminate information about American children's literature—specific books and kinds of books—and who are responsible for the building of American collections in foreign-book areas in libraries. We hope this list will be useful to teachers of children's literature in library schools and teacher-training institutions abroad and to librarians and bibliographers in research centers serving interests in foreign books for young readers. For Americans at home, the list may suggest a basis for the selection of gifts and exhibits sent abroad to represent the United States.

The worldwide translation program is expanding. It is our wish that creative writing balance or replace the overwhelming spread of mass-market books over national borders. Popularity is not excluded here; best-loved books are widely represented, particularly those we feel can best aid true education. We believe this list of exemplary titles will support UNESCO's aim to help developing countries recognize the power of the book as an essential for education, cultural enlightenment, and international understanding.

Virginia Haviland
Editor

Books for Younger Children

Picture Books

Andersen, Hans Christian. **Thumbelina.** Tr. by R. P. Keigwin. Illus. by Adrienne Adams. Scribner. 1961. 62p. $4.50.

Drawings in delicate colors portray the adventures and the enchanting, small world of the tiny heroine and turn a favorite story into a charming picture book. Ages 5–9.

Asbjørnsen, Peter C. and Jørgen E. Moe. **The Three Billy-Goats Gruff.** Illus. by Marcia Brown. Harcourt. 1957. 32p. $3.50.

The simple Norse folktale of the triumph of the three goats over the troll who attempted to eat them—dramatically enhanced by the artist. Ages 3–6.

Bemelmans, Ludwig. **Madeline.** Illus. by the author. Viking. 1939. [48]p. $3.50.

Here, as in **Madeline's Rescue** (Caldecott Medal winner) and the succeeding Madeline picture books, the inventive writer-artist follows the little boarding-school girl in delightful situations. The gay Bemelmans pictures—actual scenes in France or London—provide superb backdrops for the texts with their rhyming lines. Ages 4–7.

Bishop, Claire Huchet. **The Five Chinese Brothers.** Illus. by Kurt Wiese. Coward. 1938. [52]p. $2.50.

Loved for its repetition and gay pictures, this folktale-like story of five identical brothers shows how each with a prodigious gift outwits the executioner. Ages 4–7.

Brown, Marcia. **Once a Mouse: A Fable Cut in Wood.** Illus. by the author. Scribner. 1961. 32p. $3.50.

The Indian fable about a hermit who transforms a mouse into a tiger. Handsome three-color woodcuts. Caldecott Medal award. Ages 5–7.

Brown, Margaret Wise. **Goodnight Moon.** Illus. by Clement Hurd. Harper. 1947. [31]p. $2.95.

A favorite bedtime story, brightly pictured, shows a little rabbit and his room full of familiar toys, pictures, and clothing to each of which, one by one, he says a good-night. Ages 2–4.

Burton, Virginia Lee. **Little House.** Illus. by the author. Houghton. 1942. 40p. $3.95.

When the countryside surrounding a little house vanishes because the city expands, it doesn't seem possible that the little house will again see the stars above, a new moon coming up, or a spring day, quiet and peaceful. But it does. The colorful, superbly designed illustrations are essential to the story. Caldecott Medal award. Ages 5–8.

Burton, Virginia Lee. **Mike Mulligan and His Steam Shovel.** Illus. by the author. Houghton. 1939. 48p. $3.75.

Mike Mulligan said that his steam shovel, Mary Anne, could still dig as much in a day as a hundred men could do in a week, even if the Diesel and electric shovels were getting all the jobs. And he proved it. With full-color illustrations strong in design, this lively picture-story has become an established favorite. Ages 3–5.

Caudill, Rebecca. **A Pocketful of Cricket.** Illus. by Evaline Ness. Holt. 1964. 48p. $4.50.

A poignant, effectively illustrated story of a little boy's first day at school when it is discovered that he has brought with him his summer friend, a cricket. Caldecott Honor Book. Ages 5–8.

Chaucer, Geoffrey. **Chanticleer and the Fox.** Adapted and illus. by Barbara Cooney. Crowell. 1958. 31p. $3.75.

A skillful adaptation of Chaucer's "Nun's Priest's Tale," in which the proud cock Chanticleer, betrayed by his vanity, is carried off by the sly fox, but manages to save himself by his own wits. Striking design and color and authentic medieval details make a handsome picture book. Caldecott Medal award. Ages 5–8.

Clark, Ann Nolan. **In My Mother's House.** Illus. by Valino Herrera. Viking. 1941. 56p. $3.50.

The setting is the world of the Pueblo Indian, his people, his land, his animals, the changing seasons, his ways of life and thought. The simple text has the quality of free verse; the illustrations, in line and color, are those of an Indian artist. Ages 5–9.

Daugherty, James H. **Andy and the Lion.** Illus. by the author. Viking. 1938. 79p. $3.50.

Bold, full-page line drawings with yellow wash tell the story of small Andy who read about lions, dreamed about lions, and finally met one on the way to school—the "Androcles and the Lion" story modernized with robust humor. Each picture has one line of text. Ages 6–9.

Dayrell, Elphinstone. **Why the Sun and the Moon Live in the Sky: An African Folktale.** Illus. by Blair Lent. Houghton. 1968. 26p. $3.75.

From an early southern Nigerian collection, a brilliantly presented story about the results of an invitation to

3

Water and his following to visit the home of the Sun and Moon. Ages 5–7.

Domanska, Janina. **If All the Seas Were One Sea.** Etchings by the author. Macmillan. 1971. 32p. $4.95.

A favorite nursery rhyme, illustrated in stylized but lively fashion, comes to a climax with a great "splish-splash." Caldecott Honor Book. Ages 3–6.

Du Bois, William Pène. **Bear Circus.** Illus. by the author. Viking. 1971. 48p. $4.95.

An immediately appealing nonsense tale about the bears of Koala Park who put on a circus to entertain some friendly kangaroos who had given them a needed ride. A sequel to **Bear Party.** Ages 4–7.

Du Bois, William Pène. **Lion.** Illus. by the author. Viking. 1956. 36p. $3.75.

A Caldecott Honor Book brilliantly illustrated to tell the story of how Lion came to be "invented." Ages 5–8.

Duvoisin, Roger. **Petunia.** Illus. by the author. Viking. 1950. 32p. $3.54.

In a brightly illustrated picture book, the silly goose Petunia learns that carrying a book is not enough to make her wise. Among the happy sequels are **Petunia and the Song, Petunia Takes a Trip,** and **Petunia's Christmas.** Ages 4–7.

Duvoisin, Roger. **Veronica.** Illus. by the author. Knopf. 1952. 32p. $3.54.

In her aim to be different, a hippopotamus leaves her herd for the city, but is happy to return to her mudbank after being too conspicuous. Jolly pictures. Ages 4–7.

Emberley, Barbara. **Drummer Hoff.** Illus. by Ed Emberley. Prentice-Hall. 1967. 32p. $4.25.

"Drummer Hoff fired it off" and the cannon went "Kahbahbloom." A cumulative rhyming picture book bursting with color. Caldecott Medal award. Ages 4–8.

Emberley, Ed. **The Wing on a Flea.** Illus. by the author. Little. 1961. 48p. $3.50.
A picture book which introduces the young child to shapes—triangles, rectangles, and circles—beginning with the flea's wing and progressing to the big Ferris wheel. Blue, green, and black are used in amusing drawings on well-designed pages. Ages 5–7.

Ets, Marie Hall. **In the Forest.** Illus. by the author. Viking. 1944. [45]p. $2.50.
A little boy walking through the forest encounters small animals with whom he plays. Charmingly illustrated in paper-batik in strong black and white. Similar is a sequel, **Just Me.** Ages 3–6.

Ets, Marie Hall. **Play with Me.** Illus. by the author. Viking. 1955. 32p. $2.75.
Done in charming pastels are drawings for this simple tale of a lonely little girl eagerly searching for a playmate among the creatures of the meadow. Caldecott Honor Book. Ages 3–4.

Fatio, Louise. **The Happy Lion.** Illus. by Roger Duvoisin. McGraw-Hill. 1954. [32]p. $3.95.
A beloved inhabitant of a French zoo leaves the zoo to visit his friends—with surprising results. Further amusing adventures in **The Happy Lion Roars, The Three Happy Lions,** and other sequels introduce a compatible lioness and, later, a lion cub named François, all gaily illustrated in two colors. Ages 5–8.

Feelings, Muriel. **Moja Means One: Swahili Counting Book.** Pictures by Tom Feelings. Dial. 1971. [28]p. $4.50.

5

Unique features of African rural life and culture are shown in an unusual counting book with soft-pencil illustrations which are almost photographically realistic. Caldecott Honor Book. Ages 5–7.

Fisher, Aileen L. **Going Barefoot.** Illus. by Adrienne Adams. Crowell. 1960. 34p. $3.95.
A child, impatient to go barefoot, cries, "How soon is it to be June?" A slim picture book of humorous, imaginative verse and delicate pictures that evoke the natural world in which to observe the seasons. Ages 4–7.

Flack, Marjorie. **Angus and the Ducks.** Doubleday. 1930. 32p. $2.95.
Angus, a little black Scotch terrier, was curious about many things and thereby got into trouble. An appealing dog story with pictures full of character and humor. Ages 4–7.

Flack, Marjorie. **Ask Mr. Bear.** Illus. by the author. Macmillan. 1932. 32p. $3.50.
A tender, repetitive, wholly childlike little story about a small boy who, seeking to give his mother a birthday present, discovers the meaning of a "bear hug." Ages 3–6.

Flack, Marjorie. **The Story About Ping.** Illus. by the author. Viking. 1933. [32]p. $2.50.
Ping, a small duck on a Yangtze River houseboat, learns the folly of tardiness. Charmingly told and pictured. Ages 3–6.

The Fox Went Out on a Chilly Night. Illus. by Peter Spier. Doubleday. 1961. 44p. $3.50.
The New England countryside provides the setting for an old folk song about the wily fox who raided the farmer's barn. Drawings in brilliant autumn colors al-

ternate with sketches in black and white to illustrate the text, line by line. The simple musical arrangement is by Burl Ives. Another folk rhyme illustrated by the artist is **London Bridge Is Falling Down.** Ages 3–8.

Françoise [Seignobosc,]. **Jeanne-Marie Counts Her Sheep.** Illus. by the author. Scribner. 1957. 32p. $3.63.

In this first of a series of picture-stories set in the south of France, a little girl's anticipation of Christmas is optimistically based on the selling of her sheep's wool. Charming color illustrations. Ages 3–6.

Frasconi, Antonio. **See and Say: A Picture Book in Four Languages** [English, French, Italian & Spanish]. Illus. by the author. Harcourt. 1955. 32p. $3.25.

Colorful woodcuts show simple objects with the name of each given in the four languages. Ages 5–8.

Freeman, Don. **Corduroy.** Illus. by the author. Viking. 1967. 32p. $3.50.

Because his green corduroy overalls had one button missing, Corduroy, a winning little bear who lived in a toy shop waiting for someone to take him home, almost missed his chance. An amusing, satisfying picture book. Ages 4–8.

Freeman, Don. **Norman the Doorman.** Illus. by the author. Viking. 1959. 64p. $3.95.

Norman, a mouse dedicated to art, was doorman at a hole in the wall of the Museum of Art, but his dream was to create a work of art himself. A sophisticated picture book whose liveliness and somewhat irreverent humor pleases children and their parents. Ages 7 up.

Frog Went A-Courtin'. Retold by John Langstaff; illus. by Feodor Rojankovsky. Harcourt. 1955. 32p. $3.95.

Caldecott Medal award-winning drawings make a bright picture book of the old folk song about the difficult courtship of Frog and Miss Mousie. A companion animal-picture book in song is **Over in the Meadow**. Ages 4–8.

Gág, Wanda. **Millions of Cats.** Illus. by the author. Coward. 1938. 32p. $3.50.

A very old man and a very old woman who search for one little cat find themselves with "millions and billions and trillions of cats." A favorite story with a folk-tale quality and delightfully droll black-and-white drawings. The author-artist's **Snippy and Snappy** (about two field mice), **Nothing at All** (a puppy), and **The Funny Thing** (an animal?) are other distinctively designed picture-book nonsense stories. Ages 4–8.

Goudey, Alice E. **Houses from the Sea.** Illus. by Adrienne Adams. Scribner. 1959. 30p. $3.95.

Two children gather and identify all kinds and colors of seashells they find washed ashore on a beach. They learn that each was once a home for a small creature. **The Day We Saw the Sun Come Up,** by the same author and artist, is also beautifully illustrated in color. Ages 5–9.

Gramatky, Hardie. **Little Toot.** Illus. by the author. Putnam. 1939. 93p. $3.95.

Little Toot, the impudent tugboat, does nothing but puff, smoke, and play until the day of the big storm. Then he saves the ocean liner. Lively pictures and text recreate the bustle and stir of New York harbor. Ages 4–7.

Hoban, Russell. **Bedtime for Frances.** Illus. by Garth Williams. Harper. 1960. 32p. $3.50.

Frances, the little badger, exhibiting the familiar human characteristics of a child who at bedtime is determined to stay awake, finds innumerable excuses for attention. Pleasing sequels, illustrated by Lillian Hoban, include **Bread and Jam for Frances, A Baby Sister for Frances,** and **A Birthday for Frances.** Ages 3–5.

Hogrogian, Nonny. **One Fine Day.** Illus. by the author. Macmillan. 1971. 32p. $4.95.

The repetitive action in this retelling of an old Armenian tale shows a fox going from creature to creature and place to place to regain his tail, chopped off because of his misbehavior. Beautifully designed illustrations in warm, rich colors. Caldecott Medal award. Ages 4–7.

Holl, Adelaide. **Rain Puddle.** Illus. by Roger Duvoisin. Lothrop. 1965. 32p. $3.95.

A repetitive nursery story about silly farm animals; told with folk-tale simplicity and pictured amusingly in bright colors. Ages 3–6.

Jacobs, Joseph. **Tom Tit Tot.** Illus. by Evaline Ness. Scribner. 1965. 32p. $4.95.

The traditional tale, with pictorial interpretation that made it a Caldecott Honor Book. A further delight is the artist's interpretation of another English folk tale, **Mr. Miacca.** Ages 5–8.

Joslin, Sesyle. **What Do You Say, Dear?** Illus. by Maurice Sendak. W. R. Scott. 1958. 44p. $2.95.

Good manners and appropriate social responses are presented in an imaginative and lighthearted manner to young children, preparing them to cope with such unusual situations as bumping into a crocodile in the street or arriving by airplane for tea through a self-made hole in the roof. Amusing illustrations in black and white with blue wash. Caldecott Honor Book. A similarly gay companion is **What Do You Do, Dear?** Ages 5–8.

Kahl, Virginia. **The Duchess Bakes a Cake.** Illus. by the author. Scribner. 1955. 32p. $3.63.

The first in a popular series of rhymed picture books, this is about the Duchess, whose thirteen daughters are treated to a "lovely, light, luscious, delectable cake"—so light that it takes to the sky. Ages 4–7.

Keats, Ezra Jack. **The Snowy Day.** Illus. by the author. Viking. 1962. 32p. $3.50.

A Caldecott Medal award winner describes with full-color collage illustration the joy of a small boy's play in the snow. **Whistle for Willie,** similarly illustrated, shows how another small boy discovers how to whistle. Ages 3–6.

Leaf, Munro. **The Story of Ferdinand.** Illus. by Robert Lawson. Viking. 1939. 64p. $2.95.

Lawson's drawings do much to tell the story of the peace-loving little bull who preferred smelling the flowers to entering the bullring. Ages 5–8.

Lenski, Lois. **Little Train.** Illus. by the author. Walck. 1940. 48p. $3.25.

Engineer Small takes his train on a run. All the facts about oiling, coaling, watering, and otherwise operating a locomotive are illustrated, with brief text for each picture. Similar and much loved are **Little Airplane, Little Fire Engine,** and **Little Farm.** Ages 4–7.

Lionni, Leo. **Frederick.** Illus. by the author. Pantheon. 1966. 30p. $3.50.

A modern fable, paralleling "The Grasshopper and the Ant," in which Frederick just sits and stores sunshine while five hard-working mice prepare for winter. A fresh style of collage illustration that uses torn paper enhances the story. Caldecott Honor Book. In his earlier **Swimmy,** also a Caldecott Honor Book, paintings which are beautiful in design depict the watery deep where a small fish cleverly devises a plan for survival. Ages 3–7.

Lionni, Leo. **Inch by Inch.** Illus. by the author. Astor-Honor. 1962. 30p. $4.50.
The story of an inchworm who can measure many kinds of things but not the nightingale's song. Illustrated with handsome full-color collage pictures. Caldecott Honor Book. Ages 5–7.

Lionni, Leo. **Little Blue and Little Yellow.** Illus. by the author. Grosset. [40]p. $4.50.
An entirely original, childlike, and imaginative introduction to color in a fantasy about two blobs of color, their parents, and their playmates. Ages 5–7.

McCloskey, Robert. **Blueberries for Sal.** Illus. by the author. Viking. 1948. 54p. $3.50.
When little Sal and her mother climb one side of Blueberry Hill to pick berries and little Bear and his mother start up the other side to eat berries, there is a mix-up and the children follow the wrong mothers. The humorous blue-ink pictures are a charming complement to the text. Ages 3–6.

McCloskey, Robert. **Make Way for Ducklings.** Illus. by the author. Viking. 1941. 67p. $3.50.
The setting is Boston, but every child anywhere who has fed ducks in a pond or in a city park will take this picture book to his heart. The sepia crayon drawings have vitality in design and execution. Caldecott Medal award. Ages 3–6.

McCloskey, Robert. **Time of Wonder.** Illus. by the author. Viking. 1957. 63p. $3.95.
A distinctive, full-color picture book evokes different moods of sunshine and moonlight, fog and hurricane as

hours, days, and seasons change on a small Maine island. Caldecott Medal award. Ages 7 up.

Mayer, Mercer. **A Boy, a Dog and a Frog.** Dial. 1967. 32p. $2.50.
A hilariously funny story told without words. Ages 5–7.

Mizumura, Kazue. **The Emperor Penguins.** Illus. by the author. Crowell. 1969. 35p. $3.75.
With grace and charm but without sacrifice of accuracy the author's illustrations invest a simple yet absorbing account of the habits and habitat of the Antarctic Emperor penguin. Ages 4–8.

Mizumura, Kazue. **If I Built a Village.** Illus. by the author. Crowell. 1971. 32p. $4.50.
A charming statement on ecology in the poetically expressed ideas of a child about a world in which the people "care and share with all living things the land they love." The pictures are simple, yet striking. Ages 4–7.

Ness, Evaline. **Josefina February.** Illus. by the author. Scribner. 1963. 32p. $4.37.
Evocative woodcuts, in three colors, add distinction to this moving story of a little Haitian girl who makes a big sacrifice. Ages 5–8.

Ness, Evaline. **Sam, Bangs and Moonshine.** Illus. by the author. Holt. 1966. 48p. $3.95.
Three-color illustrations, both realistic and stylized, convey the atmosphere of a seaside setting and the imaginative fictions of Sam (short for Samantha) who learns through near-tragedy the dangers of confusing truth and "moonshine." Caldecott Medal award. Ages 4–7.

Old Mother Hubbard and Her Dog. Illus. by Paul Galdone. McGraw-Hill. 1960. 32p. $3.95.

The full nursery rhyme is enhanced by spirited black-and-white pictures touched with red. Ages 4–7.

Perrault, Charles. **Cinderella.** Illus. by Marcia Brown. Scribner. 1954. 32p. $4.50.

A Caldecott Medal award-winning retelling, with a strong fairy-tale atmosphere in its color drawings. Among other folktales also freshly and individually interpreted by this artist are **Dick Whittington and His Cat, Puss in Boots, Stone Soup,** and **The Flying Carpet.** Ages 5–8.

Politi, Leo. **Little Leo.** Illus. by the author. Scribner. 1951. 30p. $4.37.

Based on the author's own childhood, a colorfully pictured story about a little boy in Indian chief suit who comes from San Francisco to live in an Italian village. Ages 4–7.

Raskin, Ellen. **Nothing Ever Happens on My Block.** Illus. by the author. Atheneum. 1966. 30p. $2.95.

A little boy, complaining of boredom, sits dully without noticing the high drama about him—not even the burning house nor the parachute landing. A highly original picture book with bright, humorous illustrations. Ages 6–8.

Rey, Hans Augusto. **Curious George.** Illus. by the author. Houghton. 1941. 55p. $3.75.

The little monkey, George, one of the most popular characters in American picture books, has but one bad fault—an inexhaustible curiosity. There are many amusing sequels with further innocent mischief perpetrated by George, and **Cecile G. and the Nine Monkeys,** in which a lonely giraffe befriends some homeless monkeys. Ages 4–8.

Sawyer, Ruth. **Journey Cake, Ho!** Illus. by Robert McCloskey. Viking. 1953. 45p. $3.25.

A variant of the johnny cake folktale, in picture-book format. Simple crayon pictures, full of action, show how the Journey Cake rolls away, with Johnny, the cows, the ducks, the sheep, the pigs, and the donkey running after. Ages 5–8.

Sendak, Maurice. **In the Night Kitchen.** Illus. by the author. Harper. 1970. 40p. $4.95.

Bold illustrations by this world-acclaimed artist support the fantasy of Micky's dream—an adventure in the baker's night kitchen. Ages 5–7.

Sendak, Maurice. **The Nutshell Library.** Illus. by the author. Harper. 1962. 4v. $3.95.

Four miniature boxed volumes are humorously illustrated (each available also in larger format): **Alligators All Around,** an alphabet book; **Chicken Soup with Rice,** a book of rhymes; **One Was Johnny,** a counting book; and **Pierre,** a cautionary tale, about a boy who said "I don't care." Ages 3–6.

Sendak, Maurice. **Where the Wild Things Are.** Illus. by the author. Harper. 1963. 40p. $3.95.

A childlike playfulness pervades this original fantasy about a little boy's adventures with deliciously grotesque monsters. Caldecott Medal winner. Ages 4–8.

Seuss, Dr. [pseud. of Theodor Seuss Geisel]. **And to Think that I Saw It on Mulberry Street.** Illus. by the author. Hale. 1937. 32p. $3.21.

The earliest, and one of the most original, of the many "Dr. Seuss" creations describes what the imaginative Marco saw on his way home from school. Ages 4–7.

Seuss, Dr. [pseud. of Theodor Seuss Geisel]. **The 500 Hats of Bartholomew Cubbins.** Illus. by the author. Vanguard. [47]p. $2.95.

Another early "Dr. Seuss" picture book, the amusing story of a boy who could take off his hat before the King. Ages 5–7.

Shulevitz, Uri. **One Monday Morning.** Illus. by the author. Scribner. 1967. 40p. $4.95.

A small boy in a New York tenement is visited by royalty sumptuously garbed as on playing cards. Original in treatment, with well-executed, softly colored drawings. Ages 3–7.

Sleator, William. **The Angry Moon.** Illus. by Blair Lent. Little. 1970. 45p. $4.95.

Based on an Alaskan Indian legend and illustrated in glowing full-color paintings which are elaborations on original Tlingit motifs, this is the tale of a boy's rescue of his friend, held prisoner by the moon because she laughed at its ugly face. Caldecott Honor Book. Ages 5–8.

Slobodkina, Esphyr. **Caps for Sale: A Tale of a Peddler, Some Monkeys & Their Monkey Business.** Illus. by the author. W. R. Scott. 1947. [42]p. $3.75.

A gaily pictured, popular tale which succeeds notably as a story to be shared with groups of small children—about a cap peddler who takes a nap under a tree full of clever monkeys. Ages 4–7.

Steig, William. **Amos & Boris.** Illus. by the author. Farrar. 1971. [32]p. $4.50.

A handsomely produced, fable-like story about the friendship between Amos, a seagoing mouse, and Boris, his whale-rescuer, whose life in turn Amos later succeeds in saving. Superb beach scenes and rolling seascapes. Ages 4–7.

Steig, William. **Sylvester and the Magic Pebble.** Illus. by the author. Windmill. 1969. [32]p. $4.95.

Sadness comes to the Duncan parents (they are donkeys) when young Sylvester, a pebble-collector, accidentally turns himself into a stone. The large pictures in full color are evocative of the story's happiness, humor, grief, and final joy. Caldecott Medal award. **Roland the Minstrel Pig** conveys a similar charm in its animal fantasy. Ages 4–7.

Titus, Eve. **Anatole.** Illus. by Paul Galdone. McGraw-Hill. 1956. 32p. $3.95.

Unified text and drawings tell the humorous story of a French mouse who earns self-respect as well as food for his family by becoming the self-supporting First Vice President in Charge of Cheese Tasting for M. Duval's cheese factory. Followed by the equally amusing and dramatic **Anatole and the Cat** and **Anatole and the Thirty Thieves,** as well as other titles. Ages 5–7.

Tresselt, Alvin. **White Snow, Bright Snow.** Illus. by Roger Duvoisin. Lothrop. 1947. 33p. $3.75.

The feeling of a snowy world is caught in an unpretentious narrative and a sequence of winter-crisp pictures of children, falling snow, snowmen, and snow houses. The color is high-keyed and clean, the pages well-designed. Caldecott Medal award. Ages 4–6.

Tworkov, Jack. **The Camel Who Took a Walk.** Illus. by Roger Duvoisin. Dutton. 1951. [32]p. $3.95.

A beautiful young camel on an early morning walk foils the plans of a tiger and other animals. Duvoisin's illustrations have strong, flat colors and his usual humor. Ages 4–7.

Udry, Janice M. **The Moon Jumpers.** Illus. by Maurice Sendak. Harper. 1959. 30p. $3.95

Children, touched by moon magic, dance barefoot and play games among the shadows on a summer lawn. A book of atmosphere and contrasts, with its dreamlike quality enhanced by luminous pictures in tones of violet and green. Caldecott Honor Book. Ages 3–7.

Ungerer, Tomi. **Crictor.** Illus. by the author. Harper. 1958. 32p. $3.95.

Crictor, the boa constrictor, adjusts nicely to life as a pet for Madame Bodot. Tongue-in-cheek humor, Gallic atmosphere, and effective line drawings with green-and-red wash. **Emile,** just as imaginative, tells of a benevolent octopus. Ages 6–9.

Ungerer, Tomi. **Zeralda's Ogre.** Illus. by the author. Harper. 1967. 32p. $3.95.

Even the most horrendous child-eating ogre can reform—if he meets a pitying cook with little Zeralda's skill. Another delight is Ungerer's equally colorful **The Three Robbers.** Ages 5–8.

Waber, Bernard. **The House on East 88th Street.** Illus. by the author. Houghton. 1962. 48p. $3.50.

This bright picture book and its sequel **Lyle, Lyle Crocodile,** as well as other Lyle stories, have amusing make-believe about an amiable crocodile found in a city apartment bathtub. Ages 4–7.

Ward, Lynd. **The Biggest Bear.** Illus. by the author. Houghton. 1962. 84p. $3.75.

A Caldecott Medal winner with strong lithograph illustration in black and white for an imaginative story of a boy who loved the bear cub he met and adopted. Ages 6–9.

Yashima, Taro [pseud. of Jun Iwamatsu]. **Crow Boy.** Illus. by the author. Viking. 1955. 37p. $3.50.

17

The poignant story of a shy Japanese child whose great gift is mimicking the sound of crows. Handsomely illustrated. Ages 7–11.

Yashima, Taro [pseud. of Jun Iwamatsu]. **Umbrella.** Illus. by the author. Viking. 1958. 30p. $3.50.

The day Momo became three she received an umbrella and red rubber boots; but, alas, she had to wait many days for rain. Both the rhythmic text and the pictures have distinction as they express the immediate world of a small child. Caldecott Honor Book. Ages 4–6.

Zemach, Harve. **The Judge.** Illus. by Margot Zemach. Farrar. 1969. [46]p. $4.50.

"An untrue tale" concocted in rhyming nonsense to show the downfall of a judge who fails to listen to his prisoners. A bit in the style of Hogarth are the comic pictures in harmonious colors. Ages 5–8.

Zemach, Harve. **Mommy, Buy Me a China Doll.** Adapted from an Ozark children's song. Illus. by Margot Zemach. Follett. 1966. 32p. $4.95.

A cumulative folk song with repetition of nonsense in a chain of action and humorous pictures. Ages 5–7.

Zemach, Harve, ed. **Too Much Nose: An Italian Tale.** Illus. by Margot Zemach. Holt. 1967. 40p. $3.95.

A rollicking tale of three sons and three gifts; a change from the familiar folktale pattern shows the second son saving the fortunes of all with magic, nose-growing figs. Ages 5–7.

Zion, Gene. **Harry the Dirty Dog.** Illus. by Margaret Bloy Graham. Harper. 1956. 32p. $3.50.

A picture-book favorite—about a runaway dog whose increasing dirtiness prevents his being recognized at home. Equally entertaining sequels include **No Roses for Harry** and **Harry By the Sea.** Ages 4–7.

First Reading

Averill, Esther. **Fire Cat.** Illus. by the author. Harper. 1960. 63p. $2.50.

For newly independent readers, an "I Can Read" book about a cat that proves useful to a fire-engine crew. Ages 6–7.

Lobel, Arnold. **Frog and Toad Are Friends.** Illus. by the author. Harper. 1970. 64p. $2.50.

An amusing but simple "I Can Read" book, with easy vocabulary, charming illustrations, and primer format for a beginner reader. Caldecott Honor Book. Ages 4–8.

Minarik, Else H. **Little Bear.** Illus. by Maurice Sendak. Harper. 1957. 63p. $2.50.

The first of the publisher's "I Can Read" books, for beginning readers, with charming three-color drawings describing Little Bear's imaginative play adventures. Caldecott Honor Book. Followed by **Father Bear Comes Home, Little Bear's Friend, Little Bear's Visit,** and **A Kiss for Little Bear.** Ages 6–7.

Myrick, Mildred. **The Secret Three.** Illus. by Arnold Lobel. Harper. 1962. 64p. $2.50.

An "I Can Read" book in which three boys who form a club have fun deciphering a code message found in a bottle. See also the author's **Ants Are Fun**, a "Science I Can Read Book," also illustrated by Lobel. Ages 6–7.

Selsam, Millicent. **Benny's Animals and How He Put Them in Order.** Illus. by Arnold Lobel. Harper. 1966. 61p. $2.50.

The story of a boy with a penchant for neatness who asked the museum to help him put his pictures of animals in proper order. A "Science I Can Read Book." Ages 4–8.

Seuss, Dr. [pseud. of Theodor Seuss Geisel]. **The Cat in the Hat.** Illus. by the author. Random. 1957. 61p. $1.95.

The first of the "Beginner Books," in limited vocabulary, with typical Dr. Seuss drawings. Ages 6–7.

Books for Older Children

Fiction

Alexander, Lloyd. **The Book of Three.** Holt. 1964. 217p. $3.95.

Inspired by legends of ancient Wales, the author has created Prydain, mythical land of kings and villains, in which Taran, an Assistant Pig-Keeper, becomes a hero. Four sequels include **The Castle of Llyr, The Black Cauldron, Taran Wanderer,** and **The High King,** the last winning the Newbery Medal award and the National Book Award. Each part of the chronicle sees confrontations between the forces of good and evil as Taran pursues his quest to find the truth about himself. Ages 9–12.

Alexander, Lloyd. **The Marvelous Misadventures of Sebastian.** Dutton. 1970. 208p. $5.95.

The swift-paced comic adventures of an eighteenth-century court fiddler who comes to own a magical violin, his encounters with a cat accused of witchcraft and his meeting with a runaway princess. Ages 9–13.

Andersen, Hans Christian. **Seven Tales.** Tr. from the Danish by Eva Le Gallienne. Illus. by Maurice Sendak. Harper. 1959. 127p. $3.95.

Andersen stories which appeal to younger children are given added interest by many Sendak paintings in full color. Ages 8–10.

Annixter, Jane and Paul. **The Runner.** Illus. by Paul Laune. Holiday. 1956. 220p. $3.50.
A teen-age boy, recovering from polio on a Wyoming ranch, secretly tames and captures a beautiful, young wild stallion. A dramatic and sensitive picturing of animal nature and the conflicts of a boy determined to tame a wild horse. Ages 11 up.

Armstrong, William H. **Sounder.** Harper. 1969. 116p. $3.95.
The shattering experiences of a black sharecropper's family—the father's severe sentence for the theft of food and the maiming of the great dog Sounder. Newbery Medal award. Ages 12–15.

Atwater, Richard and Florence. **Mr. Popper's Penguins.** Illus. by Robert Lawson. Little. 1938. 138p. $3.50.
A house painter's interest in polar exploration leads to a gift to him of one penguin, then two—and an unexpected alteration of the Popper family's way of life. Memorable drawings enhance the comedy. Ages 8–11.

Babbitt, Natalie, **Kneeknock Rise.** Illus. by the author. Farrar. 1970. 96p. $3.95.
Gentle humor and a warm folk feeling pervade this tale of a village agreeably terrorized by the "Megrimum" of Kneeknock Rise, an illusion more believable than actual, and of the lad who solved that mystery to the discomfiture of the villagers. Newbery Honor Book. Ages 8–12.

Babbitt, Natalie. **The Search for Delicious.** Illus. by the author. Farrar. 1969. 167p. $3.95.

A fantasy in which a twelve-year-old boy's quest for the meaning of the word *delicious* frames a more heroic search for a magic whistle which will save the kingdom. Ages 9–11.

Barringer, D. Moreau. **And the Waters Prevailed.** Illus. by P. A. Hutchinson. Dutton. 1956. 188p. $4.95.

A sensitive, stimulating story of Stone Age man—particularly of young Andor, undersized but possessing a greater than usual ability to reason, who predicted to his scoffing people that a flood would come in over land where now lies the Mediterranean Sea. Ages 11 up.

Bonham, Frank. **Durango Street.** Dutton. 1965. 190p. $3.95.

Teen-age gangs, gang fights, and the life of blacks in a city housing project are convincingly drawn in a story that creates an understanding of some of the reasons for delinquency. Ages 12–16.

Brink, Carol Ryrie. **Caddie Woodlawn.** Illus. by Kate Seredy. Macmillan. 1935. 270p. $4.95.

In this biographical story of the Woodlawn family on the Wisconsin frontier in 1864, when Indian raids were dreaded, lively, red-headed Caddie and her six brothers and sisters had the courage to warn the Indians of an impending white man's attack on their village. Newbery Medal award. Ages 10–12.

Burch, Robert. **Queenie Peavy.** Illus. by Jerry Lazare. Viking. 1966. 159p. $3.50.

Queenie, at thirteen, is a thorny problem to herself and everyone else in her southern rural community until she accepts the fact of her father's shiftlessness and gives herself a chance. An appealing story with excellent characterization, convincing dialogue, and vivid setting. Ages 10–13.

Burnford, Sheila. **The Incredible Journey.** Illus. by Carl Burger. Atlantic-Little. 1961. 145p. $4.50.

Three unusual but devoted companions—a Siamese cat, an elderly bull terrier, and a young Labrador retriever—undertake a private odyssey homeward across 250 miles of rugged terrain in the Canadian northland. A tale of courage, humor, and sturdy individualism which appeals to animal-lovers. Ages 10 up.

Butterworth, Oliver. **The Enormous Egg.** Illus. by Louis Darling. Atlantic-Little. 1956. 187p. $4.25.

The fantastically humorous problems of a twelve-year-old boy who tries to raise a baby dinosaur hatched from a hen's egg. Ages 8–12.

Byars, Betsy. **Midnight Fox.** Illus. by Ann Grifalconi. Viking. 1968. 157p. $4.50.

About a sensitively portrayed city boy, reluctantly visiting in the country, who discovers the unexpected fascination of wildlife after glimpsing a black fox on his aunt's farm. Ages 9–12.

Byars, Betsy. **Summer of the Swans.** Illus. by Ted Co-Conis. Viking. 1970. 142p. $3.95.

The perceptive story of a fourteen-year-old girl whose concern for a retarded younger brother helps her see her own adolescent problems in perspective. Newbery Medal award. Ages 10–14.

Cameron, Eleanor. **A Room Made of Windows.** Illus. by Trina Schart Hyman. Atlantic-Little. 1971. 271p. $5.95.

A deftly written story of self-centered Julia, aiming to become a writer, whose relationships with family and neighbors of all ages bring her to a greater maturity and understanding of others. Ages 10–14.

Cameron, Eleanor. **A Spell Is Cast.** Illus. by Beth and Joe Krush. Atlantic-Little. 1964. 271p. $3.95.

The intense experiences of a lonely orphaned girl who, after capricious changes in her situation, finds an answer to her desperate craving for life as a member of a family. Ages 10–13.

Cameron, Eleanor. **Wonderful Flight to the Mushroom Planet.** Illus. by Robert Henneberger. Atlantic-Little. 1954. 214p. $3.75.

Highly original science fantasy in which two boys journey by space ship to a planet of spore people. Among several sequels, **Time and Mr. Bass** continues the adventures with a dramatic conflict between good and evil. Ages 9–12.

Carlson, Natalie Savage. **The Family under the Bridge.** Harper. 1958. 99p. $3.95.

The sometimes humorous, always warm and real story of a widowed mother and her three children who are befriended by a Paris tramp after he finds them usurping his private refuge by the Seine. Ages 8–10.

Carlson, Natalie Savage. **The Happy Orpheline.** Illus. by Garth Williams. Harper. 1957. 96p. $3.95.

Brigitte, one of twenty contented orphans in a home outside Paris, particularly wishes not to be adopted. Told with humor and flavor and with a lively complement of pen-and-ink sketches. Amusing sequels are **Orphelines in the Enchanted Castle** and **A Brother for the Orphelines.** Ages 7–10.

Caudill, Rebecca. **Tree of Freedom.** Illus. by Dorothy Bayley. Viking. 1949. 279p. $3.50.

Settling on rich Kentucky land in 1780 brings thirteen-year-old Stephanie and her hardworking brother, already in conflict with their father's motive in moving, into a new life of dealing with Indians, war rumors, and rigors of the wilderness. Told with an unusual depth of characterization as well as drama. Ages 12–15.

Clapp, Patricia. **Constance: A Story of Early Plymouth.**
Lothrop. 1968. 255p. $4.50.

Realistic details of the life and loves of a pretty young
girl in early Plymouth Colony flavor this substantial,
lively chronicle, told by the heroine herself. National
Book Award nominee. Ages 12–14.

Cleary, Beverly. **Beezus and Ramona.** Illus. by Louis Darling. Morrow. 1955. 159p. $3.95.

The plight of nine-year-old Beezus afflicted with an
uninhibited, imaginative little sister. In the equally entertaining **Ramona the Pest,** that five-year-old enters
kindergarten. Ages 7–9.

Cleary, Beverly. **Henry Huggins.** Illus. by Louis Darling.
Morrow. 1950. 155p. $3.95.

The first in a popular series about a small boy and his
dog Ribsy whose everyday adventures make delightfully
amusing reading. Followed by the equally entertaining
Henry and Ribsy, Ribsy, and others. Ages 8–10.

Cleary, Beverly. **Mouse on the Motorcycle.** Illus. by Louis
Darling. Morrow. 1965. 158p. $3.95.

Original make-believe in a tale of friendship between
the boy Keith and a mouse named Ralph whose mania
for Keith's toy motorcycle leads to reckless adventure.
Followed by **Runaway Ralph.** Ages 8–10.

Cleaver, Vera and Bill. **Ellen Grae.** Illus. by Ellen Raskin.
Lippincott. 1967. 89p. $2.95.

The wildly colorful tales fabricated by this imaginative
young heroine lead the community to distrust her in a
situation when, painfully, she asserts her integrity. Real
and touching and tinged with humor. Ages 9–13.

Cleaver, Vera and Bill. **Where the Lilies Bloom.** Lippincott.
1969. 174p. $3.50.

After her father's death, fourteen-year-old Mary Call Luther becomes the family head, working hard with her brother and sisters to gather and sell medicinal plants in a desperate attempt to remain together and independent. A sharp, distinctive picture of southern mountain life. Ages 10–13.

Coatsworth, Elizabeth. **The Cat Who Went to Heaven.** Macmillan. 1958. 62p. $4.95.
A Newbery Medal award winner, first published in 1930—the poetic, legend-like story of a poor Japanese artist and his "good-luck" cat that watches him paint a picture commissioned for a Buddhist temple. Re-illustrated by Lynd Ward, who did the original pictures. Ages 9–12.

Coatsworth, Elizabeth. **Jon the Unlucky.** Illus. by Esta Nesbitt. Holt. 1964. 94p. $3.50.
A secret valley, unchanged through the history of Greenland, is discovered and its inhabitants served by a young Dane who, in the late nineteenth century, stumbles upon it during a blinding snowstorm. Ages 9–12.

Coolidge, Olivia. **Men of Athens.** Illus. by Milton Johnson. Houghton. 1962. 244p. $3.50.
This writer of biographies and fiction has created thirteen stories about famous and less-known figures in the Golden Age of Athens. Newbery Honor Book. Ages 13–16.

Curry, Jane L. **Beneath the Hill.** Illus. by Imero Gobbato. Harcourt. 1967. 255p. $4.50.
In a fantasy conflict between good and evil, five vacationing cousins stray over the edge of the ordinary world into adventure with the waters under the earth and the lost "Fair Folk" from Wales. Ages 9–13.

Dalgliesh, Alice. **The Courage of Sarah Noble.** Illus. by Leonard Weisgard. Scribner. 1954. 52p. $4.50.

This simply told story of a pioneer child is based on a true incident in colonial Connecticut—when a real eight-year-old Sarah had her courage severely tested as she and her father went into the Indian-inhabited wilderness to make a new home. Newbery Honor Book. Ages 8–10.

DeJong, Meindert. **Along Came a Dog.** Illus. by Maurice Sendak. Harper. 1958. 172p. $4.50.

A vivid, unforgettable picture of barnyard behavior and relationships in a suspense-filled story of a small hen who has lost her toes, a stray dog who befriends her, and a farmer whose kindliness reaches both. Newbery Honor Book. Ages 10 up. Other animal stories by DeJong include **Hurry Home Candy** and **Shadrach** (for a younger audience) which are also Newbery Honor Books and illustrated by Sendak. Notable here is the fact that both author and illustrator are American winners of the international Hans Christian Andersen Medals.

DeJong, Meindert. **House of Sixty Fathers.** Illus. by Maurice Sendak. Harper. 1956. 189p. $3.50.

Compelling and poignant is this tale of a little Chinese boy's odyssey to safety with sixty American aviators during the bombing of his country in World War II. Memorable are the boy's faith and courage and his devotion to a pet pig. Ages 10 up.

DeJong, Meindert. **Wheel on the School.** Illus. by Maurice Sendak. Harper. 1954. 298p. $4.95.

When six Dutch children set out to entice storks to their school roof for good luck, their adventures grow in excitement to involve the whole village. The characters and action are described with rare sensitivity and dramatic power. Newbery Medal award. Other distinctive stories set in the author's native Holland are **Far Out the Long Canal, The Journey from Peppermint Street** (winner of the National Book Award), and **Tower by the Sea.** All, ages 9–12.

DuBois, William Pène. **The Giant.** Viking. 1954. 124p. $3.95.

With DuBois's own fantastic drawings, this remarkable tale tells of a boy of giant size, hidden away to keep him from ridicule. **The Great Geppy** has further highflown nonsense, about a red-and-white striped horse that belongs to the famous Bott Circus. Ages 8–10.

Du Bois, William Pène. **The Twenty-one Balloons.** Viking. 1947. 179p. $3.50.

The Newbery Medal award-winning book about the hilarious adventures of Professor Sherman whose threeweek flight in his giant balloon included a stopover on the erupting island of Krakatoa. The marvels are wonderfully illustrated by the author. Ages 10–13.

Eager, Edward. **Half Magic.** Illus. by N. M. Bodecker. Harcourt. 1954. 217p. $3.75.

The first, and most humorous, of a series of modern fantasies inspired by E. Nesbit. Here a family of imaginative children discover a magic coin that grants halfwishes, transporting them to other times and scenes —though not always the full way intended. **Knight's Castle** introduces Scott's **Ivanhoe.** Ages 8–12.

Enright, Elizabeth. **Gone-Away Lake.** Illus. by Beth and Joe Krush. Harcourt. 1957. 192p. $3.

Boy and girl cousins of ten and eleven spend a happy summer in a hidden, derelict summer resort—with its two eccentric inhabitants—exploring nature and solving a mystery. **Return to Gone-Away** continues with their

29

fun in another summer. Both are written with special conviction and humor. Ages 9–12.

Enright, Elizabeth. **The Saturdays.** Rinehart. 1941. 175p. $2.50.
The four Melendy children, bored by a succession of wet Saturdays, organize a club that makes every Saturday an adventure. A lively, humorous family story set in pre-World War II New York City. Three sequels are written with the same insight and a sense of fun. Ages 10–12.

Estes, Eleanor. **The Hundred Dresses.** Illus. by Louis Slobodkin. Harcourt. 1944. 80p. $3.95.
An unforgettable story of underprivileged Wanda Petronski who, always wearing the same clean, faded dress to school, invents for her teasing schoolmates "a hundred dresses"—on paper. Ages 9–12.

Estes, Eleanor. **The Moffats.** Illus. by Louis Slobodkin. Harcourt. 1941. 290p. $3.75.
An engaging, warm, but unsentimental story of a fatherless family's inventive fun in a very real New England town. Followed by the equally entertaining **The Middle Moffat** and **Rufus M.** Ages 9–12.

Fall, Thomas. **Canal Boat to Freedom.** Illus. by Joseph Cellini. Dial. 1966. 216p. $3.50.
An indentured boy on a New York-Pennsylvania canal boat of a century past learns the meaning of courage, friendship, and human dignity through his love for a Negro freedman. Ages 8–12.

Fisher, Aileen. **Valley of the Smallest: The Life Story of a Shrew.** Illus. by Jean Zallinger. Crowell. 1966. 161p. $3.75.
With a poet's touch in relaying observations of ecology

in a Rocky Mountain valley, the author has centered on the life of the tiny shrew. A beautifully illustrated nature story. Ages 9 up.

Fitzhugh, Louise. **Harriet the Spy.** Illus. by the author. Harper. 1964. 298p. $3.95.

A precocious New York City child keeps a diary in which she records penetrating and sometimes unwelcome truths about her schoolmates and also about the adults in her life. A favorite with children, for its robust humor and the vicarious pleasure enjoyed in its picture of Harriet's uninhibited behavior. Ages 9–12.

Fleischman, Sid. **Mr. Mysterious & Company.** Little. 1962. 151p. $4.50.

The engaging story of a traveling magic show of the 1880s in which Pa (as Mr. Mysterious) runs the business and all the family take part. Other extravagantly entertaining fiction by this author includes **By the Great Horn Spoon!, Chancy and the Grand Rascal,** and **The Ghost in the Noonday Sun.** Ages 8–12.

Forbes, Esther. **Johnny Tremain.** Houghton. 1943. 256p. $3.95.

An injury to his hand ruined Johnny's dream of becoming a famous silversmith, but it turned him into a courier for the Boston Sons of Liberty at the beginning of the American Revolution. Successfully integrated with Johnny's story are the historical facts and a vivid recreation of life in the 1770s. Newbery Medal award. Ages 12–15.

Fox, Paula. **How Many Miles to Babylon?** Illus. by Paul Giovanopoulos. David White. 1967. 117p. $3.95.

A black boy in Harlem, running away from loneliness after his mother is hospitalized, finds himself in a frightening adventure with a gang of young dog thieves. Ages 9–11.

Fritz, Jean. **Early Thunder.** Illus. by Lynd Ward. Coward. 1967. 255p. $4.95.

Both sides of the war movement are treated objectively in this story of a young boy in colonial New England just before the American Revolution. In a story of the later Civil War, **Brady** describes how a boy worked to help free slaves on the Underground Railroad in 1836. Ages 11–14.

Gage, Wilson [pseud. of Mary Q. Steele]. **Dan and the Miranda.** Illus. by Glen Rounds. World. 1962. 127p. $3.50.

Ten-year-old Dan aims to turn his spider-watching curiosity and excitement into a science fair project, but learns that scientific record-keeping demands more than enthusiasm. Lively in both story and illustration. Ages 9–12.

Gage, Wilson [pseud. of Mary Q. Steele]. **Mike's Toads.** Illus. by Glen Rounds. World. 1970. 93p. $3.95.

When extrovert Mike commits his older brother to the job of taking care of a friend's seven toads, his generosity backfires and he becomes toad-sitter himself. Humor and nature lore are delightfully combined. Ages 8–10.

Gannett, Ruth Stiles. **My Father's Dragon.** Illus. by Ruth C. Gannett. Random. 1948. 86p. $2.95.

The nonsensical adventures of "My Father," Elmer Elevator, who went off to a small island to rescue a dragon. Ages 5–9.

George, Jean C. **My Side of the Mountain.** Illus. by the author. Dutton. 1959. 178p. $3.95.

Calling into play all his resources of humor, ingenuity, and endurance, Sam Gribley manages to carry through his experiment of "living off the land" for eight months, alone, in a tree house in the Catskill Mountains. Newbery Honor Book. Ages 10–14.

Gipson, Fred. **Old Yeller.** Illus. by Carl Burger. Harper. 1956. 158p. $3.95.
This account of a fourteen-year-old settler in Texas of the 1860s and of the stray yellow mongrel who became his beloved companion vividly portrays frontier life and the spirit of a boy growing into an adult world of difficult decisions. Newbery Honor Book. **Savage Sam,** a sequel, has equal drama and humor. Ages 11 up.

Haugaard, Erik Christian. **Little Fishes.** Illus. by Milton Johnson. Houghton. 1967. 215p. $3.75.
With strength and kindness, courageous thirteen-year-old Guido battles hunger, danger, and filth as he sets out with other war orphans to find refuge at the monastery at Cassino in 1943. Ages 12–14.

Haywood, Carolyn. **Eddie and Gardenia.** Illus. by the author. Morrow. 1951. 191p. $4.75.
Eddie's goat Gardenia, because of her ungovernable appetite, is banished to his uncle's ranch in Texas—but Eddie, who accompanies her, finds she is the same hungry goat. One of the most amusing of the several "Eddie" books. Ages 7–9.

Heinlein, Robert. **Have Space Suit—Will Travel.** Scribner. 1958. 276p. $4.95.
A favorite science-fiction story, told with humor, in which a teen-age boy who gains a space suit finds himself going into outer space and becoming involved in an interspatial cold war. Ages 12 up.

Henry, Marguerite. **King of the Wind.** Illus. by Wesley Dennis. Rand McNally. 1948. 172p. $3.95.

A Newbery Medal award-winning story based on the history of the Godolphin Arabian horse that founded the thoroughbred strain of Man-o-War, and of a mute Arabian stable boy who journeyed with the horse to England. Handsomely illustrated. Another of this author's much-loved horse stories is **Misty of Chincoteague** which describes the annual round-up of wild ponies on an island off Virginia. Ages 9–13.

Hentoff, Nat. **Jazz Country.** Harper. 1965. 146p. $3.50.

A reversal of race attitudes distinguishes this unusual story of a sixteen-year-old white boy who seeks to make his way as a jazz trumpet-player with a group of black musicians in New York City. Ages 12–14.

Holman, Felice. **The Blackmail Machine.** Illus. by Victoria de Larrea. Macmillan. 1968. 182p. $4.95.

A fanciful tale in which five children and a bird-loving spinster use an airborne tree house to bargain for community action and—ultimately—world peace. Ages 9–12.

Hunt, Irene. **Across Five Aprils.** Follett. 1964. 223p. $3.95.

An unforgettable story of the impact of the Civil War on a midwestern family with divided loyalties, especially on young Jethro who must shoulder the burdens of the farm as well as the agony of brother fighting brother. Newbery Honor Book. Ages 11–14.

Hunt, Irene. **Up a Road Slowly.** Follett. 1966. 192p. $4.95.

A skillful account of talented Julie's growing up, her adjustments to her mother's death and to new patterns of life with difficult relatives. Newbery Medal award. Ages 12 up.

Johnson, Annabel and Edgar. **The Grizzly.** Illus. by Gilbert Riswold. Harper. 1964. 160p. $3.50.

The turning point in the relationship between timorous David and his father comes about during a weekend fishing trip in the Montana mountains after an enraged grizzly bear attacks and injures the father. Ages 10–13.

Johnson, Annabel and Edgar. **Torrie.** Harper. 1960. 217p. $3.95.

Tense, exciting situations, sharp characterization, and authentic background make unusually vivid this story of a journey by covered wagon to the West Coast in 1846 and a girl's growing to maturity through grim struggles for survival. Ages 11–15. For somewhat younger readers, **Bear Cat** describes a boy's involvement in mining in the West in the early 1900s.

Kelly, Eric. **The Trumpeter of Krakow.** Illus. by Janina Domanska. Macmillan. 1966. 208p. $3.95.

Fresh, handsome illustrations give a new look to this 1929 Newbery Medal award-winning story set in strife-torn Renaissance Poland, when the Charnetski family guarded the precious Tarnov crystal. Ages 12–15.

Kendall, Carol. **The Gammage Cup.** Illus. by Erik Blegvad. Harcourt. 1959. 221p. $3.95.

An exuberant fantasy about the Minnipins, a race of little people who live in a state of pleasant conformity until, threatened by the Hairless Ones, they are forced to rely on the nonconformists they have previously rejected. Ages 9–12.

Key, Alexander. **Forgotten Door.** Westminster. 1965. 126p. $3.50.

Falling onto earth from another planet, Jon, temporarily afflicted with amnesia, meets with hostility as well as with sympathy in his search for identity. Ages 10–12.

Kingman, Lee. **Year of the Raccoon.** Illus. by David Grose. Houghton. 1966. 256p. $3.50.

A penetrating story with a contemporary background, told from the viewpoint of fifteen-year-old Joey, the middle son of ordinary talents in a family of gifted and aggressive personalities. Ages 10–14.

Kjelgaard, James A. **Big Red.** Holiday. 1945. 231p. $4.50.

Danny Pickett, a trapper's son, turns a champion Irish setter into a companionable hunting partner. **Desert Dog** is another of the author's engrossing animal stories. Ages 10 up.

Konigsburg, E. L. **From the Mixed-up Files of Mrs. Basil E. Frankweiler.** Illus. by the author. Atheneum. 1967. 162p. $3.95.

Running away with her little brother because she feels unappreciated, Claudia chooses the Metropolitan Museum in New York City as an elegant hiding place and ingeniously contrives to remain hidden for several days. Newbery Medal award. Another amusing, original story is the author's **Jennifer, Hecate, MacBeth, William McKinley and Me, Elizabeth.** Ages 8–11.

Lawson, Robert. **Rabbit Hill.** Illus. by the author. Viking. 1944. 127p. $3.50.

When "New Folks" moved into the Big House on the hill, all the small animals hoped that they would be friends. A fantasy rich in invention, clear characterization, and humor, as well as in distinctive drawings by the author-artist who won a Newbery Medal for this book and an earlier Caldecott Medal for **They Were Strong and Good.** A sequel, **Tough Winter,** is equally pleasing in its picture of the special animal community on the hill. Ages 8–11.

L'Engle, Madeleine. **Meet the Austins.** Vanguard. 1960. 191p. $3.

The twelve-year-old daughter tells this contemporary story of a country doctor's family confronted with the problems of a spoiled young orphan who comes to live with them. Ages 10–14.

L'Engle, Madeleine. **A Wrinkle in Time.** Farrar. 1962. 211p. $3.95.

Spellbinding science fantasy with allegorical overtones incorporating concepts of time travel, extrasensory perception, and supernatural beings. Newbery Medal award. Ages 10–14.

Le Guin, Ursula K. **The Tombs of Atuan.** Atheneum. 1971. 163p. $5.50.

A taut, eerie, economically told fantasy which is satisfying for the richness of description of the underworld of tombs where young Arha becomes high priestess and for the drama of her escape with Ged from Earthsea. Newbery Honor Book. Ages 11–14.

Le Guin, Ursula K. **A Wizard of Earthsea.** Illus. by Ruth Robbins. Parnassus. 1968. 205p. $4.50.

The haunting tale of a quest made by an apprentice wizard who is followed by a malevolent force for evil amid the islands of an archipelago in the strange world of Earthsea. Ages 10–14.

Lenski, Lois. **Indian Captive: The Story of Mary Jemison.** Illus. by the author. Lippincott. 1941. 269p. $5.19.

Based on the historically true capture of the Jemison family by Seneca Indians in 1758. Mary, adopted to fill the place of a brave who had been killed the year before, never returned to her settlement. Ages 11–14.

Little, Jean. **Mine for Keeps.** Illus. by Lewis Parker. Little. 1962. 186p. $3.75.

Sally, a victim of cerebral palsy, faces a difficult adjustment to life at home after five years in a school for handicapped children. Other realistic family stories centered on children with problems include the author's **Take Wing** and **Home from Far.** Ages 9–12.

McCloskey, Robert. **Homer Price.** Viking. 1943. 149p. $3.
Homer Price belongs to the Tom Sawyer tradition of small boys and American humor. The hilarity of these six adventures in a midwestern setting hinges upon the gravity of telling and exaggeration in characterization and situation. Followed by the also fresh and original **Centerburg Tales.** Ages 9–13.

McGraw, Eloise J. **The Golden Goblet.** Coward. 1961. 248p. $4.95.
Daily life in ancient Thebes is seen through the eyes of Renofer, an Egyptian boy, who braves the awesome Valley of the Tombs of Kings to save a royal tomb from desecration. Adventure and mystery are skillfully blended with description of the social structure and arts and carfts of ancient Egypt. Newbery Honor Book. Ages 10–14.

Merrill, Jean. **The Pushcart War.** Illus. by Roni Solbert. W. R. Scott. 1964. 223p. $3.95.
A pseudo-serious history of a fictional war in 1976 between New York City's truck drivers and pushcart peddlers. Ages 10 up.

Miles, Miska. **Annie and the Old One.** Illus. by Peter Parnell. Atlantic-Little. 1971. 44p. $3.95.
A Navaho Indian child, loving her wise grandmother and suffering because that gay, beloved person says she is ready to die, believes in her childish way that she can prevent it. The fine ink drawings have a beauty appropriate to the text which so tenderly expresses the meaning of death. Newbery Honor Book. Ages 7–10.

Morey, Walter. **Gentle Ben.** Illus. by John Schoenherr. Dutton. 1965. 191p. $3.95.

A compelling story of the friendship between a boy and an enormous brown bear whose lives and fluctuating fortunes are interwoven. Set in a small Alaskan fishing community. Ages 10–13.

Mowat, Farley. **Owls in the Family.** Illus. by Robert Frankenberg. Atlantic-Little. 1961. 107p. $3.50.

The author draws entertainingly on his boyhood experiences in western Canada in this story of a boy whose parents allowed him to add two owls to his collection of wild pets. Ages 8–12.

Neville, Emily. **It's Like This, Cat.** Illus. by Emil Weiss. Harper. 1963. 180p. $3.95.

The thoughts, emotions, and activities of an adolescent boy in contemporary New York City are revealed in a perceptively written narrative. Newbery Medal award. Ages 12–15.

Nordstrom, Ursula. **The Secret Language.** Illus. by Mary Chalmers. Harper. 1960. 167p. $2.95.

An imaginative story of two eight-year-old girls at boarding school—one quietly homesick, the other a rebel—who find happiness in the invention and use of a secret language. Ages 8–10.

North, Sterling. **Rascal, a Memoir of a Better Era.** Illus. by John Schoenherr. Dutton. 1963. 189p. $4.50.

Looking back to his rural Wisconsin boyhood, the author recalls an idyllic and adventurous year spent with Rascal, his mischievous pet raccoon. Newbery Honor Book. Ages 11 up.

O'Brien, Robert C. **Mrs. Frisby and the Rats of NIMH.** Illus. by Zena Bernstein. Atheneum. 1971. 233p. $5.95.

The story of a widowed mouse mother seeking help for her youngest child is woven together with the story of laboratory mice and rats (including her husband) used by the National Institute of Mental Health. Ingenious, credible, and sometimes moving—a Newbery Medal award-winner. Ages 8–12.

O'Dell, Scott. **The Black Pearl.** Illus. by Milton Johnson. Houghton. 1967. 140p. $3.75.

A great black pearl, secured in a brave dive by young Ramón Salazar in Mexican waters inhabited by the dreaded giant ray, El Manta Diablo, seems to be a cause of bad luck, but there are greed and superstition as well. Legendlike and perhaps symbolic, the story projects a lingering atmosphere. Ages 12 up.

O'Dell, Scott. **Island of the Blue Dolphins.** Houghton. 1960. 184p. $3.75.

Karana, a young Indian girl who survived for eighteen years on an island off the California coast, tells the story of how she created a life for herself. Based on historical records. Newbery Medal award. Ages 10 up.

O'Dell, Scott. **The King's Fifth.** Houghton. 1966. 264. $3.95.

Graphic historical fiction in which a prisoner awaiting trial by Spain recounts his adventures as a young map-maker with the conquistadores. These chapters alternate interestingly with a record of the trial itself. Newbery Honor Book. Ages 12–15.

O'Dell, Scott. **Sing Down the Moon.** Houghton. 1970. 137p. $3.75.

A Navaho Indian girl's story of the 1860s and her tribe's forced 300-mile journey from their lands to imprisonment in Fort Sumner evokes sympathy for her people and admiration for her own remarkable courage and steadfastness. Newbery Honor Book. Ages 12 up.

Parrish, Ann. **Floating Island.** Illus. by the author. Harper.
1930. 265p. $4.95.
A highly original, suspenseful, and fun-filled story of a
shipwrecked doll family and their adventures in an island
jungle. Ages 8–12.

Rankin, Louise. **Daughter of the Mountains.** Illus. by Kurt
Wiese. Viking. 1948. 191p. $3.50.
A strong atmosphere of country shrouds the long
journey over a mountain pass made by a Tibetan girl to
the coast of India in search of her stolen dog. Written by
one well acquainted with the background. Ages 10–13.

Rawlings, Marjorie Kinnan. **Secret River.** Illus. by Leonard
Weisgard. Scribner. 1955. 51p. $3.31.
A tale of special appeal to the younger child about a
magical day in the life of little Calpurnia and her dog
Buggy-horse when they discover a "secret river" in their
Florida forest. Newbery Honor Book. Ages 7–10.

Rawlings, Marjorie Kinnan. **The Yearling.** Illus. by N. C.
Wyeth. Scribner. 1938. 428p. $6.
Portrayed here is the drama of a boy's growing-up in
the lonely, scrub country of Florida, his relationship with
an understanding father, and the crisis of his deep love
for a pet fawn. Pulitzer Prize. Ages 12 up.

Ritchie, Rita. **The Golden Hawks of Genghis Khan.** Illus.
by Lorence F. Bjorklund. Dutton. 1958. 191p. $3.75.
A search made by a young boy of Samarkand for the
special breed of hawks developed by his father leads him
through many dangers to the court of Genghis Khan. A
story exceptional for its vivid evocation of the thirteenth
century. Ages 12 up.

Robertson, Keith. **Henry Reed, Inc.** Illus. by Robert Mc-
Closkey. Viking. 1958. 239p. $3.
Carrying out a summer assignment, Henry Reed has

an eventful time organizing projects illustrating free private enterprise. Carried out with the help of the girl next door and in the interest of science, these include many diverting situations described as if recorded in Henry's own lively journal and illustrated with entertaining McCloskey drawings. More of Henry's inventive fun is found in sequels, including **Henry Reed's Baby-Sitting Service** and **Henry Reed's Big Show.** Ages 10–13.

Rounds, Glen. **The Blind Colt.** Illus. by the author. New ed. Holiday. 1960. 80p. $4.50.

Ten-year-old Whitey adopts and trains a blind colt in spite of his uncle's doubts. An enduring favorite. Ages 10–11.

Sandoz, Mari. **The Horsecatcher.** Westminster. 1957. 192p. $3.50.

A peace-loving Indian boy wins an honored place in his tribe, working against tradition and family feeling to prove his skill as a horsecatcher. A story that gives an authentic and poetic view of American Indian life of long ago. Ages 12–16.

Sauer, Julia L. **Fog Magic.** Viking. 1943. 107p. $3.50.

A little girl in Nova Scotia through her love of the fog finds adventure in a village lost for a hundred years. Enhanced by Lynd Ward's decorations. Ages 9–12.

Schaefer, Jack W. **Old Ramon.** Illus. by Harold West. Houghton. 1960. 102p. $3.25.

A young boy, learning the business of sheepherding from a wise old shepherd, gains much emotionally from the dignity and happiness of the relationship. Newbery Honor Book. Ages 10–13.

Selden, George [pseud. of George Selden Thompson]. **The**

Cricket in Times Square. Illus. by Garth Williams. Farrar. 1960. 151p. $3.95.

Chester, a country cricket, who is accidentally carried in a picnic basket to Times Square in New York City, becomes a musical sensation after he is befriended by a young boy, a mouse, and a cat. Ages 8–11.

Seredy, Kate. **The Good Master.** Viking. 1935. 120 p. $4.

A timeless, universal story of a spoiled, headstrong girl from Budapest who is gentled by the wisdom and kindness of the farm relatives she visits. Charmingly illustrated by the author, who grew up in Hungary. Ages 9–12.

Snyder, Zilpha K. **The Egypt Game.** Illus. by Alton Raible. Atheneum. 1967. 215p. $3.95.

Resourceful, imaginative children of different ethnic backgrounds play the "Egypt game" after school following their discovery of a battered reproduction of the famous bust of Nefertiti. **The Headless Cupid** presents more lively children in a story of Amanda and her new stepbrothers and stepsisters who join her in "studying" the occult. Both are Newbery Honor Books. Ages 10–12.

Speare, Elizabeth G. **The Witch of Blackbird Pond.** Houghton. 1958. 249p. $3.75.

The author pictures vividly the colonial scene of Puritan Connecticut where impulsive young Kit from sunny Barbados finds herself accused of witchcraft after she befriends a lonely old woman. Newbery Medal award. Another vivid colonial story is **Calico Captive.** Ages 10–14.

Sperry, Armstrong. **Call It Courage.** Illus. by the author. Macmillan. 1940. 95p. $4.50.

A dramatically illustrated legend-based story about a Polynesian boy who conquers his fear of the sea by making a lone canoe journey to a sacred island visited by cannibals. Newbery Medal award. Ages 10–13.

Spykman, E. C. **A Lemon and a Star.** Harcourt. 1955. 214p. $3.95.

A family of four motherless children in the early 1900s lead an ebullient, unconventional life of fun. With further adventures, **Terrible, Horrible Edie** centers on the youngest, now ten, while **Edie on the Warpath** sees her in the next year battling to vindicate her sex. Ages 10–13.

Steele, William O. **The Lone Hunt.** Illus. by Paul Galdone. Harcourt. 1956. 178p. $3.75.

An authentic frontier story of 1810 when a twelve-year-old boy made the kill on the last buffalo hunt. Another such story, **Flaming Arrows** tells of Indian raids on the wilderness settlements. Ages 10 up.

Steele, William O. **The Perilous Road.** Illus. by Paul Galdone. Harcourt. 1958. 191p. $3.50.

Young Chris was perplexed by his older brother's joining the army for the "other side" in this fast-moving Civil War story set in Tennessee mountain country. Ages 10–12.

Stolz, Mary S. **A Dog on Barkham Street.** Illus. by Leonard Shortall. Harper. 1960. 184p. $2.95

A realistic family story shows how Edward's likable, but irresponsible, Uncle Josh helps him to overcome his fears and realize his dream of having a dog of his own. Succeeded by **The Bully on Barkham Street.** Ages 8–11.

Stolz, Mary S. **The Noonday Friends.** Harper. 1965. 182p. $3.95.

A perceptive story, set in New York City, centers on Franny, whose humiliations because of poverty are offset by her happy relationships with a small brother and a best friend who belongs to a large Puerto Rican family. Newbery Honor Book. Ages 10–12.

Taylor, Theodore. **The Cay.** Doubleday. 1969. 137p. $3.50.
Human understanding, endurance, and survival are beautifully woven into this taut tale of a blinded boy and an old West Indian seaman cast by shipwreck onto a barren Caribbean island. Ages 11–14.

Thurber, James. **Many Moons.** Illus. by Louis Slobodkin. Harcourt. 1943. 47p. $3.75.
An original fairy tale of a princess who wanted the moon and a court jester who got it for her. The watercolor illustrations are an integral part of the book. Caldecott Medal award. Ages 6–9.

Ullman, James Ramsey. **Banner in the Sky.** Lippincott. 1954. 252p. $4.50.
The author's own experiences and details of the first ascent of the Matterhorn form the basis for this gripping fiction about the boy, Rudi Matt, who succeeds in conquering the mountain on which his father lost his life. Newbery Honor Book. Ages 12–14.

White, E(lwyn) B(rooks). **Charlotte's Web.** Illus. by Garth Williams. Harper. 1952. 184p. $3.95.
Now considered a classic, this farmyard fantasy immortalizes the unusual relationship between a spider, a pig, and a little girl. By a winner of the National Medal for Literature. The Garth Williams illustrations are also notable. Ages 8–12.

White, E(lwyn) B(rooks). **Stuart Little.** Illus. by Garth Williams. Harper. 1952. 184p. $3.95.
Described with charm, humor, and poignancy are the

far-more-than-mouse-size exploits of Stuart, mouse son born to an American family. The drawings greatly enhance the story. Ages 8–12.

White, E(lwyn) B(rooks). **The Trumpet of the Swan.** Illus. by Edward Frascino. Harper. 1970. 210p. $4.50.
A witty and captivating fantasy, interwoven with impeccable nature lore, about a trumpeter swan without a voice who learns to read and write and play a trumpet. Ages 9–11.

Wier, Ester. **The Loner.** Illus. by Christine Price. McKay. 1963. 153p. $3.75.
A migrant boy finds a name, a new way of life, and a permanent home in Montana sheepherding country. Newbery Honor Book. Ages 11–14.

Wilder, Laura Ingalls. **Little House in the Big Woods.** Illus. by Garth Williams. Harper. New ed. 1953. 237p. $2.75.
The first in the series of "Little House" books—about Laura and her sisters, and Ma and Pa—which depict their hard work, simple pleasures, and struggles to survive natural catastrophes, all lightened by family unity and love. Seven succeeding volumes carry Laura to young adulthood. Six of the eight are Newbery Honor Books. Ages 8–12.

Wojciechowska, Maia. **Shadow of a Bull.** Illus. by Alvin Smith. Atheneum. 1964. 165p. $4.25.
Manolo, son of the great Juan Olivar, is torn between loyalty to his village's expectation that he will follow his father in the bullring and his own secret passion to become a doctor. A moving, colorful story of Andalusian life. Newbery Medal award. Ages 10–14.

Wuorio, Eva-Lis. **Save Alice!** Holt. 1968. 165p. $3.95.

It was just as they were passing through Customs from France to Spain that the old woman thrust a big birdcage into James's lap and hissed, "Save Alice!"—Alice being a squawking cockatoo. A madly humorous tale. Ages 9–13.

Yashima, Taro [pseud. of Jun Iwamatsu] and Hatoju Muku. **The Golden Footprints.** Illus. by Taro Yashima. World. 1960. 50p. $2.95.
    The compassionate story of a small Japanese boy who witnesses nightly how parent foxes of a trapped cub visit the trap and work to free the little fox. Beautiful brush drawings in black. Ages 8–12.

Folklore

Aardema, Verna. **Tales for the Third Ear from Equatorial Africa.** Illus. by Ib Ohlsson. Dutton. 1969. 96p. $4.95.
    Well-told, easy-to-read tales from the Hausa, Ashanti, and Masai African peoples—about the adventures of crafty Anansi the spider, Tricksy Rabbit, and other dwellers of the plains and jungle. Ages 8–10.

Aardema, Verna. **Tales from the Story Hat.** Illus. by Elton Fax. Coward. 1960. 72p. $3.69.
    Clever animal tales, easily read. These and the stories in **More Tales from the Story Hat** are told by African storytellers from Sierra Leone to the Congo. Ages 7–10.

Belpré, Pura. **The Tiger and the Rabbit, and Other Tales.** Illus. by Tomie de Paola. Lippincott. 1965. 127p. $3.93.
    New tales and fresh illustration have been added to this tellable Puerto Rican collection published first in 1946. Ages 8–12.

Blair, Walter. **Tall Tale America.** Illus. by Glen Rounds. Coward. 1944. 262p. $3.96.

The heroes of American folklore have a unique quality, their exaggerated adventures and ingenuities belonging to the conquest of a new and spacious land. Here are tales of thirteen regional work giants, from Captain Stormalong, the seafarer, to Pecos Bill, the cowboy. Ages 11–14.

Bryan, Ashley. **The Ox of the Wonderful Horns and Other African Folk Tales.** Illus. by the reteller. Atheneum. 1971. 41p. $5.95.

Presented for easy reading, and handsomely illustrated with strong black-red-and-tan pictures in African style, are four amusing stories of animal trickery and a longer tale about a boy who solves his problems with the aid of a magic ox. Ages 6–9.

Chase, Richard. **Jack Tales.** Houghton. 1943. 201p. $3.95.

American versions of tales about Jack, that ubiquitous hero of folk tales, who always emerges triumphant, either through quick wit or sheer good luck. Also, **Grandfather Tales; American-English Folk Tales**—more folklore gathered by Chase from southern-mountain storytellers. Ages 9–12.

Courlander, Harold. **The Piece of Fire, and Other Haitian Tales.** Illus. by Beth and Joe Krush. Harcourt. 1964. 128p. $3.50.

Simple, humorous, well-told West Indian tales about animals, men, and gods. Ages 9–12.

Courlander, Harold. **Terrapin's Pot of Sense.** Illus. by Elton Fax. Holt. 1957. 125p. $3.27.

American Negro folk stories, including animal and tall tales, gathered firsthand from rural areas in the American South. Ages 9–12.

Courlander, Harold and George Herzog. **The Cow-Tail Switch, and Other West African Stories.** Illus. by Madye Lee Chastain. Holt. 1947. 143p. $3.27.

An authentic and attractive volume of African tales. Other lore collected and edited by Courlander with native tellers: with Albert Kofi Prempeh, **The Hat-Shaking Dance and Other Tales from the Gold Coast**—a compilation of Anansi stories; and, with Azekiel A. Eshugbayi, **Olode the Hunter, and Other Tales from Nigeria** —Yoruba and Hausa stories. Ages 9–12.

Credle, Ellis. **Tall Tales from the High Hills, and Other Stories.** Illus. by Richard Bennett. Nelson. 1957. 156p. $3.50.

From the southern mountains of the United States come these entertaining—occasionally slapstick—and always vivid tales. Ages 8–12.

Gillham, Charles E. **Beyond the Clapping Mountains: Eskimo Stories from Alaska.** Illus. by Chamimun. Macmillan. 1943. 134p. $3.95.

Simple animal folk tales characteristic of Alaska, as told to the author by Eskimos. Line drawings by an Eskimo girl. Ages 9–10.

Guirma, Frederic. **Tales of Mogho: African Stories from Upper Volta.** Illus. by the author. Macmillan. 1971. 113p. $4.95.

Eight humorous fables from West Africa's oral tradition, as recorded for the first time and translated from the French by this reteller who is a United Nations officer. Ages 9–12.

Haviland, Virginia. **Favorite Fairy Tales Told in Poland.** Illus. by Felix Hoffmann. Little. 1963. 90p. $3.25.

These faithful versions of five traditional tales are enhanced by a distinguished artist's interpretations on pages designed for easy reading. Others in this series of "Favorite Fairy Tales" include selections from Denmark, illustrated by Margot Zemach, and from Italy, illustrated by Evaline Ness. All, ages 7–10.

Irving, Washington. **The Legend of Sleepy Hollow.** Illus. by Leonard Everett Fisher. Watts. 1966. [58]p. $3.75.

A handsomely illustrated edition of the classic tale of Ichabod Crane and the Headless Horseman. Ages 11–14.

Kelsey, Alice Geer, reteller. **Once the Hodja.** Illus. by Frank Dobias. McKay. 1943. 170p. $3.59.

Humorous tales from Turkey, about Nasr-ed-Din Hodja who is both wise and foolish. **Once the Mullah** centers on the Persian counterpart of this folk character. Ages 9–12.

McCormick, Dell J. **Paul Bunyan Swings His Axe.** Caxton. 1936. 111p. $3.50.

American legends of lumbering, about the giant woodsman and his great blue ox. Ages 8–12.

Marriott, Alice Lee, comp. **Winter-telling Stories.** Illus. by Richard Cuffari. Crowell. 1969. 82p. $3.95.

Ten Kiowa Indian stories about Saynday, who made the world the way it is, who sometimes did good and sometimes made trouble. (Originally publ. in 1947.) Ages 9–12.

Nic Leodhas, Sorche [pseud. of Leclaire Alger], ed. **Heather and Broom.** Illus. by Consuelo Joerns. Holt. 1960. 120p. $3.07.

Eight enchanting tales capture the lilt of language, subtle humor, and haunting atmosphere of the Scottish highlands. The author includes a statement of sources and background for each story. **Thistle and Thyme,** Newbery Honor Book, illustrated by Evaline Ness, contains ten more magical and humorous tales. **Ghosts Go Haunting,** illustrated by Nonny Hogrogian's woodcuts, and **12 Great Black Cats and Other Eerie Scottish Tales,** illustrated by Vera Bock, contain additional tellable tales of the supernatural. All, ages 9–12.

Pyle, Howard. **Some Merry Adventures of Robin Hood of Great Renown in Nottinghamshire.** Scribner. 1883. 212p. $2.95.

A dozen of the stories based by Pyle on classic ballads were here adapted by him to a shorter, more easily read form but retain the style, spirit, and famous drawings of his longer book. Ages 10–13.

Sherlock, Philip. **Anansi, the Spider Man: Jamaican Folk Tales.** Illus. by Marcia Brown. Crowell. 1954. 112p. $3.

West Indian tales about Anansi, the West African hero "who was a man when things went well, but who became a spider when he was in danger." Drawings capture the gaiety and humor. Ages 9–12.

Singer, Isaac Bashevis. **Zlateh the Goat and Other Stories.** Illus. by Maurice Sendak. Harper. 1966. 90p. $4.50.

A choice volume of seven Jewish tales from middle Europe, superbly told and illustrated. All ages.

Tashjian, Virginia. **Once There Was and Was Not: Armenian Tales Retold.** Based on stories by H. Toumanian. Illus. by Nonny Hogrogian. Little. 1966. 85p. $4.50.

A satisfying collection of stories about common folk, gods, and giants. The illustrations are in full harmony. **Three Apples Fell from Heaven** is a sequel. Ages 7–10.

Thompson, Vivian L. **Hawaiian Myths of Earth, Sea, and Sky.** Illus. by Leonard Weisgard. Holiday. 1966. 83p. $3.95.

A dozen creation stories with Polynesian gods and heroes. Handsome three-color illustration. Ages 9–12.

Poetry

Frost, Robert. **You Come Too: Favorite Poems for Young Readers.** With wood engravings by Thomas W. Nason. Holt. 1959. 94p. $3.50

A slim volume of poems, out of Frost's "simplicity, wisdom, and humanity." All ages.

Jones, Hettie, compiler. **The Trees Stand Shining: Poetry of the North American Indians.** Illus. by Robert Andrew Parker. Dial. 1971. 32p. $4.95.

Full-color paintings accompany these short haiku-like North American Indian poems which were originally chanted as songs. Ages 8 up.

Sandburg, Carl. **Early Moon.** Illus. by James Daugherty. Harcourt. 1930. 136p. $3.95.

Sandburg says of himself, "some days I am in the mood for the prairie, the skies, the trees. On other days I can feel the noise, the jumble and the confusion of the city." This slender collection of free verse, American in flavor, sensitive, personal in vision, has appeal for today's youth. A later volume, **Wind Song,** contains 16 newer poems as well as many of the earlier ones. An introduction offers the poet's fine explanation of poetry. Ages 12 up.

Biography

Aulaire, Ingri M. and Edgar P. d'. **Abraham Lincoln.** Illus. by the authors. Doubleday. Rev. ed. 1957. 55p. $3.95.

A short picture-story of Lincoln's life, covering the period from his birth to the close of the Civil War, with anecdotes emphasizing the honesty, humor, and tolerance of this great president of the United States. Simple enough for eight-year-olds, it is of interest to any age. Caldecott Medal award. Presented in similar format are **George Washington, Christopher Columbus, Leif Eriksson,** and **Benjamin Franklin.** Ages 8–10.

Coolidge, Olivia. **Gandhi.** Houghton. 1971. 278p. $5.95.

A moving portrayal of the man whose long life was spent in a total effort to improve conditions for the people of India and whose philosophy of *satyagraha*—resistance by nonviolence—was to have meaning for other countries as well. Ages 13 up.

Coolidge, Olivia. **Tom Paine, Revolutionary.** Scribner. 1969. 213p. $3.95.

A thoroughly researched portrait of a man first hailed as a hero of the American Revolution and then rejected by those who had admired him; a depiction also of the spirit of the late 1700s. Ages 12 up.

Daugherty, James H. **Daniel Boone.** With original lithographs in color by the author. Viking. 1939. 94p. $4.50.

A biography, written with a sense of the dramatic, in simple narrative catches the spirit of the wilderness frontier. The illustrations are bold and romantic. Newbery Medal award. Other distinctively illustrated, faithful biographies written in this artist's robust prose style are **Poor Richard** (Benjamin Franklin) and **Abraham Lincoln.** Ages 11–14.

Dewey, Anne P. **Robert Goddard, Space Pioneer.** Little. 1962. 154p. $4.50.

About the man who built and fired the first liquid-fuel

rocket and the people who encouraged and helped him. Historic photographs illustrate the text and add interest. Ages 12–15.

Fisher, Aileen and Olive Rabe. **We Alcotts.** Illus. by Ellen Raskin. Atheneum. 1968. 278p. $4.95.
A fictionalized biography of the Alcott family, freshly presented from the viewpoint of the mother of the "Little Women." Ages 12–14.

Hautzig, Esther. **The Endless Steppe: Growing Up in Siberia.** Crowell. 1968. 243p. $4.50.
The story, directly and simply told, of Esther's five arduous childhood years in Siberia during enforced exile from Poland in World War II. Ages 11 up.

Latham, Jean L. **Carry On, Mr. Bowditch.** Illus. by John O'Hara Cosgrave II. Houghton. 1955. 251p. $3.50.
A lively, fictionized biography of Nathaniel Bowditch, Salem mathematician-sailor whose book, **The American Practical Navigator,** has been a standard text for a century and a half. Illustrated by a specialist in sailing ships. Newbery Medal award. Ages 12 up.

Lisitzky, Genevieve H. **Thomas Jefferson.** Illus. by Harrie Wood. Viking. 1933. 358p. $4.13.
A clear account of the United States president whose activities and interests were so closely knit with the public life of his day that his biography becomes a presentation of the thought of the period and of the issues faced by the colonies and the young nation. Ages 12 up.

Petry, Ann. **Harriet Tubman: Conductor on the Underground Railroad.** Crowell. 1955. 247p. $3.95.
A poignant portrait of the indomitable woman called

"the Moses of her people" who, after escaping from slavery herself, led three hundred other slaves to freedom. Ages 12–16.

Rosen, Sidney. **Galileo and the Magic Numbers.** Illus. by Harve Stein. Little. 1958. 212p. $4.50.

An account of this sixteenth-century astronomer, struggling against superstition and bigotry to prove and defend his scientific ideas, makes clear why he became known later as the founder of modern experimental science. In **Dr. Paracelsus** the biographer reveals the challenge of another pioneer who fought the medical superstitions of his day. Ages 10–14.

Sandburg, Carl. **Abe Lincoln Grows Up. . . .** Illus. by the author. Harcourt. 1928. 222p. $3.95.

Reprinted from the adult book **Abraham Lincoln: The Prairie Years,** this covers young Lincoln's life up to 1831, including his family's move to the Middle West and his work on the Mississippi River. Ages 12 up.

Stafford, Marie P. **Discoverer of the North Pole: The Story of Robert E. Peary.** Illus. by Walter Buehr. Morrow. 1959. 220p. $3.95.

A first-hand account by Peary's daughter reveals how this explorer's singleness of purpose in the face of many discouraging failures and dangers ultimately led to his discovery of the North Pole. Ages 11–14.

Wood, Laura N. **Raymond L. Ditmars: His Exciting Career with Reptiles, Animals and Insects.** Messner. 1944. 272p. $3.34.

The story of the development of a boy's early interests into a career as a famous naturalist—told with humor, liveliness, and a respect for scientific observation. Ages 12–14.

Yates, Elizabeth. **Amos Fortune: Free Man.** Aladdin. 1950. 181p. $2.50.

A moving biography of a black man, born an African prince and sold in a Boston slave market when he was fifteen, who later bought his own and his wife's freedom and established himself at last, a respected citizen, in New Hampshire. Newbery Medal award. Ages 12–14.

History, Peoples, and Places

Coy, Harold. **The Americans.** Little. 1958. 328p. $4.95.

A nontextbook account of American history, in terms of how Americans have lived and dealt with their problems. Ages 12–14.

Daugherty, James. **Of Courage Undaunted: Across the Continent with Lewis and Clark.** Illus. by the author. Viking. 1951. 168p. $5.

Robust prose and drawings convey the spirit of adventure, the vision and courage, that sent Meriwether Lewis and William Clark on a two-year expedition of discovery and exploration through the Western wilderness to the Pacific in 1804–5. Ages 12–14.

Mead, Margaret. **People and Places.** Illus. by W. T. Mars and Jan Fairservis and with photographs. World. 1959. 318p. $6.95.

A noted anthropologist's study of five cultures—Eskimo, Plains Indian, Ashanti, Balinese, and Minoan—discusses the likenesses and differences among men. Numerous attractive illustrations. Ages 11–14.

Schechter, Betty. **The Peaceable Revolution.** Houghton. 1963. 243p. $3.75.

The concept of nonviolent resistance is provocatively interpreted here in discussion of ideas advanced by Thoreau and Gandhi, and their influence on those, both Negro and white, who furthered the revolt against segregation in the United States. Ages 12–15.

Sutherland, Efua. **Playtime in Africa.** Illus. by Willis E. Bell. Atheneum. 1962. 56p. $3.75.
A brief text accompanies extraordinarily alive photographs taken in Ghana to capture the universal activities and spirit of childhood. Ages 7–10.

Tunis, Edwin. **Frontier Living.** Illus. by the author. World. 1961. 160p. $6.95.
A comprehensive text and many meticulous illustrations show the spirit as well as the physical details of living in untamed areas, beginning with the early American frontiers and stretching away to the Far West of the United States. Succeeding attractive historical pictures of daily life, crafts, and implements are provided in **Colonial Living** (from earliest settlements to the Revolution) and **The Young United States, 1783–1830** (turbulent periods in growing cities and on the expanding frontiers). Ages 10 up.

Tunis, Edwin. **Indians.** Illus. by the author. World. 1959. 157p. $4.95.
Detailed drawings on every page greatly enhance this comprehensive, highly readable treatment of the life and customs of American Indian tribes before the white man's coming. Ages 10 up.

White, Anne Terry. **Prehistoric America.** Illus. by Aldren Watson. Random. 1951. 182p. $1.95.
The story of America before the arrival of the Indians —a time of prehistoric animals—which clearly reveals the excitement of discovering the evidence. Ages 10–13.

The Arts

Atwood, Ann. **Haiku: Mood of Earth.** Scribner. 1971. 31p. $5.95.

Designed to provide visual and intellectual pleasure in the poetry of nature, a full-color photograph of distinctive quality together with a black-and-white photo of a small segment of the same subject illustrate each example of the haiku poetry presented here. Ages 7 up.

Bergere, Thea and Richard. **From Stones to Skyscrapers: A Book about Architecture.** Dodd. 1960. 91p. $3.75.

A broad coverage of the development of architecture from early Egyptian to modern styles. Meticulous line drawings. Ages 10 up.

Chase, Alice Elizabeth. **Looking at Art.** Crowell. 1966. 119p. $4.50.

Profusely illustrated with color reproductions of paintings (some sculpture and prints), this illuminating text interprets artistic techniques used in different periods and stages of culture. Ages 10 up.

Commins, Dorothy B. **All about the Symphony Orchestra and What It Plays.** Illus. by Warren Chappell. Photographs by Constantine Manos and others. Random. 1961. 137p. $2.95.

A well-written and fully illustrated account of the characteristics and development of orchestral instruments, forms of music written for the orchestra, and the function of the conductor. Ages 9–13.

Downer, Marion. **Discovering Design.** Lothrop. 1947. 104p. $3.95.

Principles of design are discussed and illustrated with photographs of patterns in nature which reveal their inspiration for designs in textiles, ceramics, and other arts and crafts. Ages 10–13.

Downer, Marion. **The Story of Design.** Lothrop. 1963. 216p. $5.50.

Handsome photographs accompany discussion of examples of design in art and household objects chosen from prehistoric time to today. Ages 11 up.

Glubok, Shirley. **The Art of Ancient Egypt.** Atheneum. 1962. 48p. $5.95.

Well-reproduced photographs of wall paintings, statues, and art objects accompany text provided by a young people's lecturer at New York's Metropolitan Museum of Art. In a series that includes also similar volumes on "Lands in the Bible," ancient Greece, Rome, Peru, and Mexico, and on the art of the Eskimos and North American Indians. Ages 10 up.

Hoban, Tana. **Look Again!** Macmillan. 1971. 36p. $4.95.

A striking, sometimes amusing, and surprising photographic picture book in which blank pages with a cut-out square reveal a portion of pictures below and thus focus on the quality of the design—as, for example, a piece of a shell or the stripes of a zebra. Ages 7–10.

Hunt, Kari and Bernice Wells Carlson. **Masks and Mask Makers.** Illus. by the authors. Abingdon. 1961. 67p. $3.50.

Kinds of masks worn by man through history are interestingly described—their symbolic and social functions and the folklore and ceremonies surrounding their use. Ages 10–13.

Moore, Janet Gaylord. **The Many Ways of Seeing: An Introduction to the Pleasures of Art.** World. 1969. 141p. $7.95.

Music and literature are related to various techniques of art in their total effect of interpreting nature and humanity. A rewarding book illustrated by colored reproductions as well as black-and-white drawings. Newbery Honor Book. Ages 12–15.

Rockwell, Anne. **Filippo's Dome.** Atheneum. 1967. 82p. $3.50.

With a vivid background of fourteenth- and fifteenth-century Italy, this easily read biography of Filippo Bruneleschi shows how his brilliance and determination enabled him to complete the dome of the great cathedral in Florence. Ages 10–13.

Rockwell, Anne. **Glass, Stones & Crown: The Abbé Suger and the Building of St. Denis.** Atheneum. 1968. 80p. $3.75.

Believing that beauty would turn men toward the love of good, the Abbot Suger, a colorful figure of the Middle Ages, built the first great Gothic church in France. Ages 10–12.

Scheffer, Victor B. **The Seeing Eye.** Photographs by the author. Scribner. 1971. 47p. $5.95.

A skillful photographer's color pictures plus his brief text stimulate the child's awareness of form, color, and texture in nature, and dramatically illustrate the interrelationships of design, mathematics, and nature study. Ages 10 up.

Weiss, Harvey. **Collage and Construction.** Illus. with photographs. Young Scott. 1970. 63p. $3.95.

A practical manual, profusely illustrated, which encourages appreciation and judgment as well as skills in two- and three-dimensional crafts. Ages 9 up. Also stimulating are this craftsman's **Paper, Ink and Roller** (techniques of print-making) and **Paint, Brush and Palette** (the materials and essential techniques of painting). Ages 12 up.

Science and Nature

Branley, Franklyn M. **The Nine Planets.** Illus. by Helmut K. Wimmer. Crowell. Rev. ed. 1971. 86p. $4.50.

In a clear straightforward style this astronomer describes our solar system, devoting a short chapter to each of the nine planets. Ideas of the ancients, modern discoveries, and conflicting theories are presented. Clear illustrations and diagrams. Other books on astronomy by Dr. Branley include **The Earth: Planet Number Three.** Ages 12 up.

Bronowski, Jacob, and Millicent E. Selsam. **Biography of an Atom.** Harper. 1965. 43p. $3.95.

A brief, lucid text is supplemented by many diagrams, drawings, and photographs to reveal the structure, origin, and unchanging cycle of the carbon atom. Ages 9–13.

Brown, Lloyd A. **Map Making: The Art that Became a Science.** Little. 1960. 217p. $5.75.

An account of the scientists, astronomers, mariners, geographers, and others who tried to solve the complex problem of charting the earth's surface and helped develop "a crude form of art into an exact science." Detailed pen-and-ink sketches of early maps and instruments enhance the text. Ages 9–14.

Cosgrove, Margaret. **Strange Worlds Under a Microscope.** Illus. by the author. Dodd. 1962. 138p. $3.50.

The historical development and many aspects of a

variety of microscopes are presented with discussion of scientific principles and simple experiments. Also, **The Strange World of Animal Senses,** about the highly sensitive use of sensory perceptions in the animal kingdom. Ages 10–14.

De Borhegyi, Suzanne. **Ships, Shoals and Amphoras.** Illus. by Alex Schomburg. Holt. 1961. 176p. $3.95.

Exciting discoveries of buried treasures held by the sea: ancient Greek and Roman shipwrecks, buried cities, and Spanish treasure ships. Techniques used in this new field of underwater archaeology are described, with some of the problems confronted and some of the successes achieved. Ages 9–13.

Diggins, Julia E. **String, Straightedge, and Shadow: The Story of Geometry.** Illus. by Corydon Bell. Viking. 1965. 160p. $4.53.

Concepts of geometry in their development from earliest times are graphically illustrated. Ages 11–14.

Dowden, Anne O. T. **Look at a Flower.** Illus. by the author. Crowell. 1963. 120p. $4.50.

A well-organized scientific guide, with meticulously detailed drawings by a botanical artist. Ages 10–14.

Flanagan, Geraldine. **Window into an Egg: Seeing Life Begin.** W. R. Scott. 1969. 72p. $5.95.

A simple text and excellent close-up photographs document the continuing growth of a chick embryo, observed through a window inserted into the side of a fertile egg. Ages 9–12.

Hutchins, Ross E. **This Is a Tree.** Photographs by the author. Dodd. 1964. 159p. $3.75.

The life processes of a tree, its leaves, flowers, and seeds, plus information on tree-ring dating, wood, and other tree products. Also, **This Is a Leaf, This Is a**

Flower, and **Amazing Seeds**—all with equally handsome photographs. Ages 10–14.

Kadesch, Robert R. **The Crazy Cantilever and Other Science Experiments.** Illus. with photographs and drawings. Harper. 1961. 175p. $3.95.
Forty experiments in physics clearly illustrated by use of simple materials. Ages 10–14.

Kavaler, Lucy. **The Wonders of Algae.** Illus. with photographs and with drawings by Barbara Amlick and Richard Ott. Day. 1961. 96p. $3.69.
A well illustrated, scientific explanation of the tiny organisms which offer to the space age a source of food and medical supplies and industrial raw material. Ages 11–14.

Liers, Emil. **A Black Bear's Story.** Illus. by Ray Sherin. Viking. 1962. 192p. $3.00.
A pleasingly fictionalized, well-illustrated account of a family of black bears in the north woods of Minnesota. Also, **A Beaver's Story** and **An Otter's Story.** Ages 8–12.

Milne, Lorus, and Margery Milne. **The Crab that Crawled Out of the Past.** Illus. by Kenneth Gosner. Atheneum. 1965. 84p. $3.50.
A description of the horseshoe "crab's" antiquity of anatomy and this living fossil's unusual adaptation to environment through millions of years. Ages 9–13.

Pringle, Laurence. **One Earth, Many People: The Challenge of Human Population Growth.** Illus. with photographs. Macmillan. 1971. 86p. $4.95.
A provocative, succinct consideration of population problems facing the world today. Ages 10–16.

Ravielli, Anthony. **Adventures in Geometry.** Illus. by the author. Viking. 1959. 177p. $3.

An artist's striking study of lines and shapes in nature and in some of man's productions—a stimulating approach to the study of geometry, with a brief text and beautiful drawings which make the book an unusual aesthetic experience. Also, **Wonders of the Human Body,** an introduction to anatomy which, with montage drawings and diagrams, explains many of the miracles of the human body; and **From Fins to Hands: An Adventure in Evolution,** a dramatic study of the development of the human hand. All, ages 12 up.

Ruchlis, Hyman. **Orbit: A Picture Story of Force and Motion.** Harper. 1958, 147p. $3.95.

The laws of motion and gravitation and their application to such movements as those of automobiles and spaceships; helpfully illustrated with diagrams and photographs. Ages 10–14.

Scheele, William E. **Prehistoric Animals.** World. 1954. 125p. $6.20.

The author, Director of the Cleveland Museum of Natural History, describes important and interesting animals in the march of evolution. His drawing of each animal is accompanied by text giving size, period, locality from which fossils came, and museums where they may be seen. Excellent charts. Also, **Ancient Elephants.** Ages 12 up.

Selsam, Millicent E. **Birth of a Forest.** Illus. by Barbara Wolff. Harper. 1964. 54p. $2.95.

Photographs and explicit drawings implement a simple text to explain how a lake turns into a forest. Also, **From the Sea Came an Island** and **How To Be a Nature Detective.** Ages 9–12.

Shippen, Katherine. **Men, Microscopes, and Living Things.** Illus. by Anthony Ravielli. Viking. 1955. 192p. $3.50.

An inviting history of theories and experiments relating to living things contributed by the great biologists from earliest times to the present. Newbery Honor Book. The author's **Men of Medicine** describes great medical discoveries with similar provocativeness. Ages 12 up.

Shuttlesworth, Dorothy. **The Story of Spiders.** Illus. by Su Zan Noguchi Swain. Doubleday. 1959. 56p. $3.50.

The characteristics, habits, and appearances of many varieties of spiders are discussed in enough detail, with information about webs, nests, and nurseries, to satisfy the general reader. Many color illustrations. Another fascinating study is **The Story of Ants.** Ages 10 up.

Stefferud, Alfred. **Wonders of Seeds.** Illus. by Shirley Briggs. Harcourt. 1956. 119p. $3.25.

The life cycle of plants and unusual facts about many kinds of seeds are presented informally in storylike fashion, with suggestions of experiments to be carried out by children. Ages 10 up.

Sterling, Dorothy. **Caterpillars.** Illus. by Winifred Lubell. Doubleday. 1961. 64p. $3.50.

The habits of both moth and butterfly caterpillars, their differences, their enemies, and their means of self-preservation are described in an attractive well-organized book for young naturalists. Ages 7–10.

Ubell, Earl. **World of Push and Pull.** Photographs by Arline Strong. Atheneum. 1964. 58p. $3.25.

Drawing on familiar experiences of children, the author explains basic physical phenomena, including gravity, inertia, friction, and centrifugal force. **World of the Living** has more excellent photography, of wildlife and the balance of nature. Ages 8–10.

Directory of Publishers

Abingdon Press
  201 Eighth Ave., S.
  Nashville, TN 37202

Addison-Wesley Publishing
  Co., Inc.
  Reading, MA 01867

Aladdin
  (*See* E. P. Dutton & Co., Inc.)

Astor-Honor, Inc.
  67 Southfield Ave.
  Stamford, CT 06904

Atheneum Publishers
  122 E. 42d St.
  New York, NY 10017

Atlantic Monthly Press
  (*See* Little, Brown Co.)

Caxton Printers, Ltd.
  Caldwell, ID 83605

Coward-McCann, Inc.
  200 Madison Ave.
  New York, NY 10016

Thomas Y. Crowell Co.
  201 Park Ave. S.
  New York, NY 10003

The John Day Co., Inc.
  257 Park Ave. S.
  New York, NY 10010

The Dial Press, Inc.
  750 Third Ave.
  New York, NY 10017

Dodd, Mead & Co., Inc.
  79 Madison Ave.
  New York, NY 10016

Doubleday & Co., Inc.
  277 Park Ave.
  New York, NY 10017

E. P. Dutton & Co., Inc.
  201 Park Ave. S.
  New York, NY 10003

Farrar, Straus & Giroux, Inc.
  19 Union Square, W.
  New York, NY 10003

67

Follett Publishing Co.
  1010 W. Washington Blvd.
  Chicago, IL 60607

Grosset & Dunlap, Inc.
  51 Madison Ave.
  New York, NY 10010

E. M. Hale and Co.
  1201 S. Hastings Way
  Eau Claire, WI 54701

Harcourt Brace Jovanovich,
  Inc.
  757 Third Ave.
  New York, NY 10017

Harper & Row, Publishers, Inc.
  49 E. 33rd St.
  New York, NY 10016

Holiday House, Inc.
  18 E. 56th St.
  New York, NY 10022

Holt, Rinehart & Winston, Inc.
  383 Madison Ave.
  New York, NY 10017

Houghton Mifflin Co.
  2 Park St.
  Boston, MA 02107

Alfred A. Knopf, Inc.
  201 E. 50th St.
  New York, NY 10022

J. B. Lippincott Co.
  521 Fifth Ave.
  New York, NY 10017

Little, Brown & Co.
  34 Beacon St.
  Boston, MA 02106

Lothrop, Lee & Shepard Co.
  105 Madison Ave.
  New York, NY 10016

McGraw-Hill Book Co.
  330 W. 42nd St.
  New York, NY 10036

David McKay Co., Inc.
  750 Third Ave.
  New York, NY 10017

The Macmillan Company
  866 Third Ave.
  New York, NY 10022

Julian Messner
  1 W. 39th St.
  New York, NY 10018

William Morrow & Co., Inc.
  105 Madison Ave.
  New York, NY 10016

Thomas Nelson, Inc.
  250 Park Ave.
  New York, NY 10017

Pantheon Books
  201 E. 50th St.
  New York, NY 10022

Parnassus Press
  2422 Ashby Ave.
  Berkeley, CA 74705

Prentice-Hall, Inc.
  Englewood Cliffs, NJ 07632

G. P. Putnam's Sons
200 Madison Ave.
New York, NY 10016

Rand McNally & Co.
P.O. Box 7600
Chicago, IL 60680

Random House, Inc.
201 E. 50th St.
New York, NY 10022

Rinehart
(*See* Holt, Rinehart & Winston, Inc.)

William R. Scott, Inc.
(*See* Addison-Wesley Publishing Co., Inc.)

Charles Scribner's Sons
597 Fifth Ave.
New York, NY 10017

Vanguard Press, Inc.
424 Madison Ave.
New York, NY 10017

The Viking Press, Inc.
625 Madison Ave.
New York, NY 10022

Henry Z. Walck, Inc.
19 Union Square, W.
New York, NY 10003

Franklin Watts, Inc.
845 Third Ave.
New York, NY 10022

The Westminster Press
Witherspoon Building
Philadelphia, PA 19107

David White, Inc.
60 E. 55th St.
New York, NY 10022

Windmill Books, Inc.
257 Park Ave., S.
New York, NY 10010

The World Publishing Co.
110 E. 59th St.
New York, NY 10022

Young Scott Books
(*See* Addison-Wesley Publishing Co., Inc.)